IN THE DRIVER'S SEAT

First published in 2009 by Zest Books,
an imprint of Orange Avenue Publishing
35 Stillman Street, Suite 121, San Francisco, CA 94107
www.zestbooks.net

Created and produced by Zest Books, San Francisco, CA
© 2009 by Orange Avenue Publishing LLC

Typeset in Fournier MT

Teen Nonfiction/New Experience/Transportation / Cars

Library of Congress Control Number: 2009933013
ISBN-13: 978-0-9800732-4-9
ISBN-10: 0-9800732-4-3

CREDITS
EDITORIAL DIRECTOR: Karen Macklin
CREATIVE DIRECTOR: Hallie Warshaw
ART DIRECTOR: Tanya Napier
WRITER: Erika Stalder
ADDITIONAL RESEARCH: Nikki Roddy
GRAPHIC AND COVER DESIGN: Tanya Napier
ILLUSTRATOR: Kunkamon Taweenuch
PRODUCTION DESIGNER: Marissa Feind
MANAGING EDITOR: Pam McElroy
TEEN ADVISORY BOARD:
Atticus Graven, Lisa Macklin, Andrea Mufarreh, Trevor Nibbi, Sasha Schmitz

Printed in Canada
First printing, 2009
10 9 8 7 6 5 4 3 2 1

IN THE DRIVER'S SEAT

A girl's guide to her first car

Special thanks to our advisor Bill Mufarreh
from B&W Service Center in San Francisco

Brake and Wheel Service Center
3260 26th Street
San Francisco, CA 94110
bwservicecenter.com

For my friend Kenneth "Kenny B." Bezzant, who loved cars.

Among all of life's freedom-winning firsts, few things are more liberating than getting your first car. Along with that new set of wheels comes instant independence. *Finally*, leave events when you're good and ready, quit worrying about whether that bus will ever come, and avoid being subjected to the questionable musical tastes of other drivers. It's a grand notion—that with a turn of a key, this hunk of metal, plastic, and rubber can take you from stuck-in-a-rut captivity (or a painfully boring party) to a state of wind-in-your-hair wonder. But beyond the romance, your car is also a machine. And, like any machine, it can—and will—break down, which will leave you feeling pretty powerless if you don't know how to deal.

This book will elevate you from a clueless newbie to a total car star who refuses to be taken on a ride. Inside, you'll get the 411 on all of your car's parts and systems so that you'll know what to do when something stops working. You'll also learn how to confidently shop for a car, be taken seriously by the male-dominated auto repair industry, and perform quick fixes that will save you time (and win you street cred among your friends). And the best part is: You'll learn how to do it all on your own.

Now *that's* real freedom.

CONTENTS

1 SNAGGING YOUR FIRST CAR p11

2 LEARNING TO LOVE
(OR AT LEAST LOOK AT)
YOUR OWNER'S MANUAL p25

3 CHECKING OUT YOUR
CAR'S ANATOMY p29

4 STOCKING YOUR
CAR WITH THE
MUST-HAVES p43

5 MAINTAINING YOUR NEW SET OF WHEELS p53

8 NAVIGATING DICEY DRIVING SITUATIONS p97

9 STYLING YOUR RIDE p113

6 FIXING STUFF ON THE FLY p69

7 GOING TO THE MECHANIC p87

INDEX p122

1

SNAGGING YOUR
FIRST CAR

So you're about to get your first car.

This is one of the best things that can possibly happen to you. It's also a giant pain. Obviously, life isn't an MTV reality show in which a new Benz magically appears in the driveway as soon as a girl turns 16. For most of us, getting a car takes some work.

You may need to save up to buy a car, and then actually go shopping for one. If you get a hand-me-down, you may need to repair it. And either way, you'll need to register it, get it insured, and come up with gas money. Managing your own auto-motive affairs is a rite of passage and, like all rites of passage, it's simultaneously bitter and sweet.

This chapter is mostly about how to select your first car, so if you already have one, you can skip to page 23 to read about how to get it insured. Of course, you could also read this section for advice on what to do if, and when, you do buy a car on your own.

PAYING FOR YOUR RIDE

For most Americans, owning a car is the second biggest expense next to owning a house. You prob-

ably won't own a house anytime soon, but you may have to pay, or at least help pay, for your car. If that's the case, it's important to know what you—and your wallet—are in for.

When you pick up a wide-eyed puppy from the pound, you still have to factor in the cost of food and vet bills to keep the pup healthy. Cars are similar in that their lifetime costs go beyond the purchase price. Here are some of the expenses you should factor in when saving up for your vehicle.

- **Any repairs.** This means any immediate and potential future ones, as well as any mainte-nance—like periodic oil changes, tune-ups, and brake checks. (Once you know the exact car you intend to buy, you can budget more specifically—see Do Your Homework on page 20.)

- **Car insurance.** This is expensive for new drivers, like you, but luckily it's one of the few things in life that is cheaper for girls than for guys (unlike bathing suits and haircuts).

- **Gas costs.** You can research these by calcu-lating the gas mileage rating for that particular car, then factoring in how far you plan to travel every day.

- **Registration fees.** These vary from state to state and are usually paid annually.

- **Professional checkup.** Before you buy a car, you'll want to have a mechanic check it out to ensure you're not buying a total lemon. See page 21 for info on how to find a pro.

It may be hard to draw up an exact budget for your first year as a car owner because you don't yet know what repairs may be needed in, say, six months, but by estimating these expenses, you can at least know an idea *before* buying your first set of wheels.

COST-CUTTING CONCEPTS

1 Think basic. Car parts for luxury or sports cars (like Beamers and Rovers) cost much more than parts for simple economy cars (think Toyotas or Nissans). Generally, the simpler the car, the cheaper the parts. This will make a difference when you have your first breakdown and need repairs.

2 Think small. All cars have a set number of cylinders, typically 4, 6, or 8. Cars with the most cylinders have the most power but will also suck more gas from an engine than those with fewer cylinders.

3 Bargain. When you finally make the move to buy, whether at a dealership or through a private seller, keep in mind that prices are negotiable—so don't be afraid to offer a lower price.

FODDER FOR FIRST-TIME FINANCERS

If you are thinking about taking out a car loan, think about it very carefully. A typical car loan involves putting a lump sum of money down, then making monthly payments that include interest for the next five years or so (the longer the loan term—which is usually described in months, like 48 or 60 months—the lower your monthly payments). But borrowing money from an institution isn't quite the same as borrowing from Mom, who might forget about that fifty bucks she loaned you for that must-have makeup spree at Sephora. There's no chance a bank or dealership will forget that you owe a car payment, the exact amount you owe, or the day it's due. And if you don't pay or you pay late, there will be repercussions, specifically damaged credit (which is like a bad report card that can haunt you when you are trying to take a college or home loan, or even trying to land a job). Bottom line: Be sure you can make payments on time before taking out a loan.

If your parents are loaning you the money, respect the privilege by treating their loan just as you would a loan from a bank. Draw up a contract that includes the rate and frequency of car payments you'll give them. (Google "personal loan," "contract," and "template" for examples online.) Sign it and have your parents do the same. Each party should keep a copy.

KNOW WHAT YOU WANT

You wouldn't date just *anyone*, right? You want to be with someone you find attractive, feel comfortable around, and can depend on. The same standards apply when you choose a car.

THINK ABOUT THESE THINGS:

- Will you be using it to drive long distances? If so, make sure it gets good gas mileage, is very reliable, and is really comfortable to sit in.

- Will you need to carry other passengers, or surfboards or skis? If yes, then look for a station wagon or a car with racks on top. Alternately, if you live in a city with tough parking, make sure your car is small enough to squeeze into tight spaces.

- Do you want a car with a top-of-the-line safety ranking? Look for an airbag-equipped car with stellar crash-test records.

Consider all of these factors before buying. You have to fit well with what you are driving. At the same time, don't be *too* choosy. You can come home with the most beautiful, perfect car in the world, but if you need to spend the next three years paying it off, it's pretty much guaranteed that you will wind up hating it.

ENVIRO TIP

Eco Auto

If you want to own an eco-friendly ride, check out the Environmental Protection Agency's Green Vehicle Guide online at www.epa.gov/greenvehicles. Plug the make, model, and year of your prospective ride into the agency's calculator to find out how it rates when it comes to fuel economy, air pollution, and greenhouse-gas emissions.

SCOUT AROUND

Once you have a sense of how much you can spend and what type of car you want, it's time to go shopping! The main places to look are:

- online sources or sites run by your local newspaper

- local auto-trader publications (which can usually be picked up for free at newspaper stands) or the classified section of neighborhood newspapers

- local used-car dealers

If you know a car buff, take him or her with you. If you don't know a car buff, take someone, *anyone* with you. If you have a less emotionally invested person there to give you a second opinion, you'll be less likely to get sweet-talked by a slick salesperson or private power-seller. And remember: Don't jump on the first thing you see. Give yourself at least a few weeks of looking to really see what's out there.

CAR SMARTS

Aunt Betty's Old Beater

Sometimes, the best deals come from your social network, so ask around. You never know who might be trading in a great older car for a newer one: a parent's friend, a friend's parent, the local mechanic. Getting a used car from someone you know is great because you might get a better deal and you can generally trust them more to tell you exactly what's wrong with the car. Some folks will just give you their old car to get it off their hands. So what if it needs $2,000 worth of repairs—it's a free car! And in some states, if it's free, you also won't need to pay taxes on it at the DMV.

CHECK OUT THE GOODS

If you decide on a used car, you need to give it a good inspection before you can seriously consider buying it. Go through this checklist when inspecting the car:

✔ Look for slightly off-color paint, which could indicate that the car has undergone major body work as the result of a big accident (which could suggest there's other more serious internal damage, as well).

✔ Test the shocks (the car part that prevents your car from bouncing all over the road) by sitting on the corner of the hood. Look to see if the car bobs up and down when you get off. If so, it might need new shocks (and shocks are expensive to replace!).

✔ Check the tires (including the spare) for uneven wear or low tread. (See page 59 for instructions.)

✔ Pop the hood and check the engine oil, coolant, and brake fluid. (See pages 54-57 for instructions.) All of the fluids should look clean. White- tinged oil or rusty-looking coolant could indicate problems with the engine.

✔ Look at the expiration date on the battery to make sure it has life left in it.

✔ Turn the engine on and check the exhaust coming from the tailpipe—it shouldn't be thick, grayish black, or blue, but nearly invisible.

✔ Look at hoses under the hood (near the radiator and windshield area) for cracks, warping, or hardened spots. These conditions can mean current or future leaks in the cooling and heating systems.

✔ Look on the ground under the car to see if anything is leaking.

✔ Get inside and press every button, flip every switch, and pull every lever to make sure everything works. Don't forget:

- the heater, air-conditioning, and defroster
- the light switches
- the seat belts
- the windshield wipers
- the turn signals
- the sound system

✔ Open and close all the doors and windows, paying attention to the door-open light. Make sure it goes off when the door is shut. If it stays on, the door may not fit evenly in the frame (which could mean the car was in an accident and there is internal damage you can't see).

TEST-DRIVE IT

If your car passes your inspection, it's time to drive it. (If the owner or dealer says no, then you don't want to do business with them.) A test drive is the best way to know how you feel about the car. You might find that the not-so-appealing teal car rides the smoothest, is the most comfortable, or has the lowest amount of miles on it. Also, make sure you fit well in the car. You need to be able to comfortably see over the steering wheel, reach the pedals and controls on the dash, and have basic ease in maneuvering the car.

TO REALLY TEST A CAR'S PERFORMANCE, DO THE FOLLOWING:

- If you have a friend with you, ask him or her to stand behind the car as you inch away for your test drive. Ask your friend to note if the back wheels veer to one side or the other — this can indicate there are problems with the car's axle or hub.

- Take the car on all types of terrain—a steep hilly road, gravel, freeways, and high-traffic areas. This will give you a true sense for how the car handles—not just a sample of how it may do in a quaint, traffic-free cul de sac.

- Listen for any weird noises, vibrations, or odors.

- Make sure the brakes don't feel too soft and that the car accelerates smoothly when you press the gas.

- Finally, note the car's mileage, make, model, year, vehicle identification number (VIN), and asking price—you'll need this info to do further research.

WOMEN AT THE WHEEL

Who Said Women Can't Drive?

Next time one of your pinheaded pals makes a derogatory comment about women drivers, hit him with the facts. According to research, women are more likely to use turn signals and wear seat belts, less likely to be involved in fatal accidents, and less likely to drink and drive. This all adds up to safer and—one may argue— better driving.

CAR SMARTS

How to Fit With Your Car

Your car should not only suit your personality and needs, but it should also fit your body. Even though you're relatively inactive while driving, your joints and muscles can undergo stress from sitting improperly. Also, having poor positioning in a car puts you in greater danger if you should get into an accident. Here are some modifications to make sure that your driver's seat is perfect for you. If you are test-driving a car and you can't get comfortable, consider getting a different car.

✔ Adjust the headrest on the back of your seat so your entire head rests on the cushion. If the headrest is positioned lower, where it supports your neck, it's more likely to maximize whiplash when in an accident.

✔ The height of your seat's backrest should reach your shoulders, so raise or lower the tilt accordingly.

✔ When driving, your knees should be higher than your hips—you may need to tilt the seat up or down to achieve this position.

✔ Drive with both hands on the steering wheel to alleviate stress on your shoulders and arms.

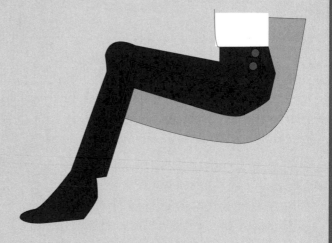

DO YOUR HOMEWORK

It helps to do a little research if you want to make an informed decision. Before or after you look at specific cars, be sure to check out these things:

✔ Look up the Kelley Blue Book price (*kbb.com*) to make sure the asking price isn't off base.

✔ See how high the car's model and make rank according to *consumerreports.org*. Also look for user and professional reviews of the car on sites like *cartalk.com*, *cars.com*, and *Edmunds.com*. If two or three sources are reporting the same flaws (faulty transmissions! bad water pumps!) with a particular car, you might want to reconsider your choice.

✔ Check the car's safety status at *safercar.gov*. It can tell you frontal, side, and rollover crash ratings for a particular vehicle and outline safety features built into the car (like air bag and head restraint specs).

✔ Calculate how much the car will cost you to operate. You can use online cost-to-own tools like those at *Edmunds.com*, *nadaguides.com*, or *autofinancing101.org*. These calculators can estimate how much you'll spend on things such as fuel, maintenance, and repairs over the course of five years or less.

✔ If buying from a private seller, ask to see the car's maintenance and repair records. At the very least, you'll want to see proof that the car has passed emissions tests, if such tests are required by your state or county. If a car can't pass these tests, it's likely it will need expensive repairs. (In most places, you won't be able to legally drive the car unless it passes an emissions inspection.)

✔ Call the US Department of Transportation's Vehicle Safety Hotline at 1-800-424-9393 or go online at *www-odi.nhtsa.dot.gov/complaints* to find out what complaints have been filed and what recalls have been made on parts for the make, model, and year of the car you're interested in purchasing.

✔ Buy a history report from *carfax.com* or *auto-check.com*. This is a report that actually says everything that has happened to the car—ever. It will tell you things the seller might not, like whether the car has been in an accident and, if so, when it was repaired and inspected. To do this, you have to have the car's vehicle identification number (VIN).

CAR SMARTS

Buyer Beware

When buying a used car from a private party, be sure to ask if there is a lien on the car. A lien is an outstanding debt from the previous owner to the bank. If there is a lien, make sure that you resolve the issue with the bank and the previous owner before you give the seller any money for the car.

HAVE IT CHECKED OUT BY A PRO

If you think you're ready to buy, send the car through one more vital test and have it examined by your family mechanic or one who specializes in that particular type of car (and who's not an in-house specialist at the dealer or the seller's buddy down the street). To find a specialty mechanic, search your local listings for "mechanic" or "auto shop" and the make of your car. It should cost about $100 for the mechanic to do a full inspection of the car. It sounds like a lot of money, but if it prevents you from buying a crappy car that you would be stuck spending $1,000 for repairs, it's worth it.

If you don't have the option to take the car off site, arrange to have a certified technician come to you and inspect the car. Hop online and search for "used-car inspections" or "prepurchase car inspections" and include the city where the car is located. It's best to contact someone who has been certified a "master technician" by the National Institute for Automotive Service Excellence.

BUY IT

You've found the right ride to buy and you're ready to do the deed. But there's more to it than writing a check or handing over your credit card.

When buying from a private seller, you'll need to follow your state's protocol for transferring title of ownership, registering the car, and fulfilling other owner and buyer responsibilities (like paying taxes through the DMV or getting a car inspected). To be sure you're on top of your game, check with your local DMV on what you'll need to do and which forms you'll have to fill out. Have the forms ready for the seller to sign if needed. Finally, even if you are buying the car from a friend, it's good to create a contract that states the agreed selling price of the car and other terms of the sale, such as whether a warranty is included or the buyer is responsible for paying for the required emissions tests. The contract doesn't have to be written by a lawyer—you can write it yourself (type in "automobile bill of sale" for sample contracts online).

The main point of the contract is to make sure everyone knows what the agreed price and terms are.

If you're buying your car from a dealership, the salesperson will likely walk you through the paperwork and formalities. Be sure to ask for a warranty on the car, whether it is new or used.

INSURE IT

Most states require drivers to have insurance and, regardless, it's a good idea to have it anyway. Insurance basically works like this: You pay a certain amount each year and are covered for some or all expenses if you should get into an accident. There are many types of insurance policies that offer a whole range of coverage (for instance, some offer coverage if your car is stolen, some offer large payments on medical bills if you are in an accident, some cover only the bare minimum). The better the coverage, the more expensive it is, so understand your options fully.

In general, insurance costs more for teens than for older drivers. After you get your car, you'll want to shop around for the best policy at the best price. Some companies will offer discounts for teen drivers who pass driver's ed or another type of safety course. Most companies also offer discounts for students with a B grade point average or better. If you get a traffic violation or have an accident, your insurance rates often go up, so when calling around, be sure to ask about the company's policy on that. Some policies include an "accidental forgiveness" clause that protects your rates from going up if you get into a minor fender bender, and that's a good thing to have.

LEARNING TO LOVE
(OR AT LEAST LOOK AT)
YOUR OWNER'S MANUAL

Every new car comes with a glove compartment-sized manual. And unlike the manuals that come with your various electronic devices, your car manual is one that you definitely want to hold on to. Even though you already know how to start and operate the car, you'll need to learn everything else about your particular ride, including the secrets to keeping your car running in perfect shape and the tricks that will help get you out of jams. Want to know where to position the jack when changing a tire? How about what type of oil your car takes? When to get your car serviced? Where everything is located under your hood? Your manual's got the goods.

The thought of wading through your car's bible can feel daunting. It contains hundreds of pages and—let's face it—is a boring read. The good news? You're not writing a research paper on it, so you don't have to read the whole thing from front to back. Instead, use these tips to cruise through it and get what you need.

- Familiarize yourself with how the contents are indexed. That will help you know where to look for what. For instance, would you find information on what type of oil your car uses under Recommended Lubricants and Fluids or under a section called Maintenance and Service? Phrasing will vary from manuel to manuel, so get familiar with the categorization used in yours.

- Scan the table of contents and locate sections that cover emergency roadside problems. You'll want to flag emergency lifesavers like where to locate the jacking point in case you need to change a tire, or how to properly push-start your car when it conks out. Mark these pages with red sticky flags to indicate that they contain emergency info.

- Thumb through the book and keep an eye out for illustrations that will help you locate vital engine system parts. Mark those pages with

CAR SMARTS

Buy the Book

If you're buying a used car, the manual might be missing. You can buy one online or from the carmaker or dealer. Some manuals can be downloaded for free, but it's best to have the actual books, since they're compact, bound, and easy to store in your car.

sticky flags of a designated color. If that deep-set rectangular part closest to the hood latch is steaming, you'll be ready to access the pictures and tell roadside assistance you have a problem with your radiator.

- Highlight useful specifications for your car, such as what type of oil it requires; what psi (pounds per square inch) the tires should be kept at; and when the car should be serviced. That way, this info will jump out at you when you're looking to perform a little maintenance.

- Now that you've extracted the most pertinent parts of your manual, run through the book again and strike out sections that discuss features that don't apply to your particular make of car (like the parts about turbo or all-wheel drive, when your model is a simpler, 2-wheel-drive version). Eliminating what's not useful will help you better find the information that is.

- Store the manual in your glove box with this book, and keep the two together at all times.

The Need for Speed

Around the time when women were just settling into the workplace, Shirley Muldowney headed to the racetracks. She was the first woman to drag-race her way past 250 mph, and by 1982 she had become the first person—man or woman—to win the Winston World Championship three times. For more on the hot-shot racer, check out the 1983 film depicting her rise to the top, Heart Like a Wheel.

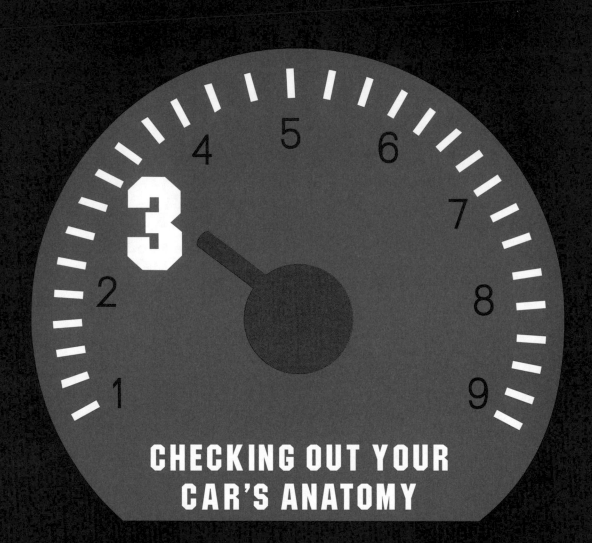

3

CHECKING OUT YOUR CAR'S ANATOMY

Trying to understand what's under
the hood of a car can be overwhelming at first. All those parts.
All that metal. To the untrained eye, all that stuff can look like
a pile of leftover marching band instruments that have been
fused into one unsightly hunk of monochromatic twists and
turns. And then there are all of the controls inside the car, and
the brake and exhaust systems underneath. You take anatomy
courses in school, right? Well, this is kind of like that. Except
there aren't boy and girl cars.

Getting to know your new car and its parts is crucial if you want
to be able to care for it and also speak your mechanic's language
when you take it into the shop. If you can talk the talk, a repair
person will be less likely to write you off as a clueless girl while
billing you for fixes you don't need or charging you double for
ones that you do.

UNDER THE HOOD

Whether you have an SUV or a classic VW, remember that different cars have the same basic working parts under the hood—though the layout and configuration of these parts can vary slightly. For instance, in some cars the engine block (that big hunk of metal in the middle) is parallel to the dashboard line. In others, it's perpendicular.

To start, crack open your car's manual and flip to the diagram of all the parts located under the hood. As you locate the various parts, find them in the manual to see what they do.

CAR SMARTS

Popping the Hood

To see what's under the hood, you need to know how to get it open—which is something they don't teach you in driver's ed. To pop the hood, first pull the release lever, which is typically somewhere below the steering wheel on the left. You'll see the hood bounce up a bit. Then, go to the front of the car and search for the lever in between the slightly raised hood and the rest of the car. When you find it, pull either toward you or push it to the side (depending on your car) and wait for the hood to release. Prop up the hood by sliding the long metal rod that runs along either the right side or across the front into the small hole in the underside of the hood.

push latch up or to the side

FLUIDS

Our bodies and our planet need plenty of fluid to keep everything running smoothly. The same holds true for your car. Different fluids for brakes, the engine, transmission, power steering, cooling system, and windshield wipers are vital to keeping all the parts under your hood and in your car moving. Dehydrate your engine of oil and you risk overheating, and even destroying, the entire engine system. Each type of fluid is generally housed in a plastic reservoir under the hood. Some can be accessed by a screw-top lid, others are reachable by dipstick, and all are marked with a label on top. Here's the basic 411 on your car's fluids. See pages 54-55 for info on how and when to check fluid levels.

Brake fluid—also called hydraulic fluid, this syrup-like lubricant pushes the brake pads against the rotors when you step on the brake, causing the car to stop. When brake fluid is low, the brake pedal will extend really far down when you step on it, and it will take more pressure to make the brakes work. (See pages 39-40 for information about brakes). Worn brake pads can also cause the brake fluid level to sink. The brake fluid is inside a short, round reservoir.

Windshield washer fluid—the blue stuff that cleans your windshield. You can keep it full in summer but never more than two-thirds full in winter because the fluid expands if it freezes. It's in a deep plastic container with little wipers on the cap.

Coolant—a neon-colored mixture of water and antifreeze (a chemical substance that prevents the water from freezing) that cycles through the radiator, thermostat, and water pump to keep the engine system at the right temperature. It's housed in a plastic container.

Engine oil—the syrupy-colored oil that lubricates your engine and keeps it running smoothly can be found on top of the engine and is accessed through the oil filler cap. Nearby is the engine oil dipstick, which is a long, thin metal wand that reads how much engine oil is in the car. The end of the stick will have "min" and "max" marks to help you judge whether oil should be added.

WOMEN AT THE WHEEL

Female Inventors
Think men invented all things automotive? Think again. Look at what female inventors have dreamed up: windshield wipers (patented by Mary Anderson), the turn signal (invented by actress Florence Lawrence), the material used for radial tires known as Kevlar (invented by chemist Stephanie Kwolek), and the "turn signal turner offer"— the device that stops the signal after you've made your turn (invented by high school senior Laurie DiStefano as part of a class assignment!).

Transmission fluid— fluid that lubricates all the working parts inside your transmission and keeps the system running clean. Some cars will feature transmission fluid dipsticks, which makes checking fluid levels easy. If you're driving around with a low level of transmission fluid, it can cause your car's gears to shift incorrectly. Its reservoir sits out of sight, beneath other parts under your hood.

Power steering fluid—this reddish-pink liquid lubes the parts located near the axles to help turn the wheels with ease. It's housed in a round reservoir on top of the engine near the fan belts.

ENGINE AND CONNECTING PARTS

Once you've singled out the fluid reservoirs, you're left with a maze of metal parts, plastic housings, and rubber tubes. These are the car's main parts, which work together to keep your ride running and at a proper temperature. If your car starts acting up, it's likely due to a failure in one or more of these parts. It's crucial to know what each thing is and what it does so you understand what your mechanic is talking about when he/she says, "We're gonna have to drop in a new alternator and run a diagnostic on your battery." Most of these parts can be easily identified if you compare what you see to the diagram in your manual.

Air filter—a contraption with super-thin paper that catches dirt, dust, bugs, and other yuck before passing  the air along to the engine to mix with fresh fuel. It's located inside a plastic case that is sometimes round and other times rectangular and is usually on or near the engine block.

Drive belts—rubber belts that look like giant rubber bands stretched around various round pulleys to power different mechanisms in the car.

Some cars have two belts:

1. a **fan belt** (a belt with rugged teeth that powers the radiator fan and other accessories)

2. a **timing belt** (a belt with rugged teeth that ensures the engine is running at the right rhythm)

Some cars have only one belt, which does the whole job:

1. a **serpentine belt** (a flat belt that propels it all—the fan, the **alternator**, **water pump**, and other engine accessories)

Check your manual to see how your car is configured.

Alternator—a round hunk of metal equipped with lots of air vents that converts mechanical energy to electricity to charge the **battery** and power the lights, stereo, and other electrical accessories.

Fuel injector—a valve that dispenses fuel into the **intake manifold**, where the fuel is burned and thus able to power the **engine.** Most cars have more than one fuel injector as part of its fuel injection system.

Fuel filter—a filter that removes gunk from the fuel so clean gas is delivered to the **fuel injectors.**

CV boot—a rubber accordion-like cover on the left and right half ends of the axles that transfers power from the **transmission** to the **axles** and wheels.

Hoses—rubber tubes that carry fluids to different systems in your car. A heater hose moves heat to your windshield to help defrost it in the winter. **Radiator hoses** carry fresh coolant to and hot coolant away from the **radiator.**

Intake manifold—a cluster of aluminum pipes perched on top of the **engine block** (looks like a rack of ribs) that funnels a mixture of fresh air and fuel through the **engine's** system.

Engine—a hefty hunk of metal from which all energy is dispersed. The engine can either be installed parallel or perpendicular to the windshield line. It works to power the **transmission,** which in turn powers the wheels to get you moving.

Exhaust manifold—connected metal pipes that provide a pathway for burned gas to go from the engine to the **catalytic converter,** and then through the rear pipe under the car, into the **muffler,** and out the **exhaust pipe.**

Catalytic converter—a metal piece, hidden from view, that looks like a flattened soda bottle. It filters out exhaust for cleaner tailpipe emissions.

Battery—a black box that provides electricity to the ignition and starting systems so that your car will start when you turn the key.

Transmission—a large cylinder-shaped machine that is responsible for the change in power and speed when you change gears and drive up and down hills. It is sometimes coupled with the **differential** to make a part called the transaxle.

Power steering pump—a pump powered by the **serpentine belt** that makes it easier to turn your steering wheel.

COOLING SYSTEM

The cooling system's parts are located in the front section of the hood nearest to the headlights and grill. The cooling system uses electricity to power a fan, various pumps, a radiator, and other parts, which work together to remove heat from the engine and stabilize your car's temperature.

Radiator—a rectangular unit with several wavy slats. It removes heat from the passing water and coolant so the engine won't run too hot.

Water pump—with the aid of a spinning pulley, this paddle wheel picks up coolant and pushes it through the motor to cool the **engine**.

Upper and lower radiator hoses—hoses that transport the coolant back and forth between the **water pump** and the **radiator**.

Thermostat—a part that regulates the flow of the coolant in the **engine** so the engine runs at a consistent temperature.

UNDER THE CAR

It's one thing to pop a hood and look underneath, but it's a little harder to get under your car to see what's going on. Luckily, you don't have to. Most cars have a pretty similar frame that supports the brake system and the muffler. Have a look at this illustration, as well as the one in your owner's manual, to identify what's going on under your car.

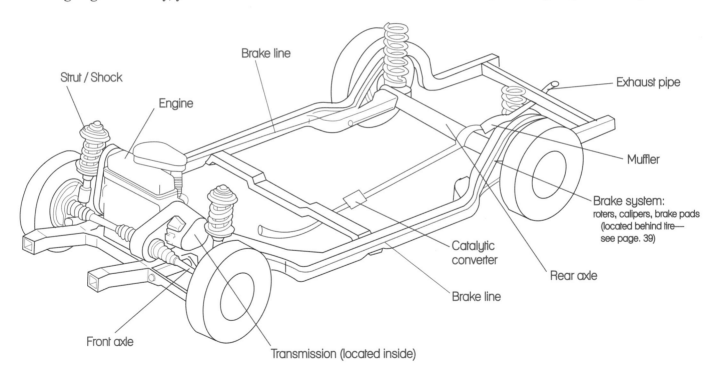

Strut / Shock

Engine

Brake line

Exhaust pipe

Muffler

Brake system:
roters, calipers, brake pads
(located behind tire—
see page. 39)

Catalytic
converter

Rear axle

Brake line

Front axle

Transmission (located inside)

EXHAUST SYSTEM

Muffler—a device attached to the **exhaust pipe** that is equipped with a hollow tube or two and protrudes from beneath your car in the back. It quiets noise from the exhaust system.

Exhaust pipe—a pipe that provides a pathway for burned gas to travel to the **muffler.**

Shocks and struts—parts that contain springs to help soften the blow of a bumpy ride by absorbing road shock. Shocks and struts help keep your car from bouncing and bottoming out.

BRAKE SYSTEM

Rotors—metal discs the size of a small pizza are attached to the **axles** and give **brake pads** something to grab onto in order to slow or stop the car.

Calipers—these C-shaped clamps squeeze against the brake pads, putting pressure on the **rotor,** therefore stopping the car.

Brake pads—coated metal pads to help slow or stop the car when pressure is applied.

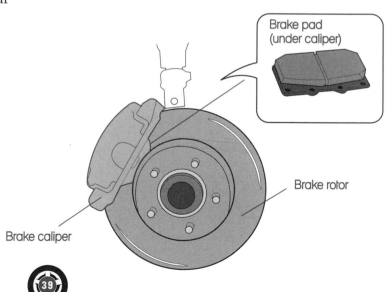

Brake pad
(under caliper)

Brake rotor

Brake caliper

Master cylinder—a device that pushes brake fluid to the front and back of the car through the **hydraulic line**, causing the **brake pads** to jam against the **rotors** and stop or slow your car.

Hydraulic line (brake line)—tubing that runs from the master cylinder to each wheel on the car, carrying the brake fluid.

Differential—a system of gears that allows the wheels to rotate at different speeds when turning a corner.

OTHER PARTS

Frame—a metal skeletal system that protects the driver from accidents.

Axles—rods that help the wheels rotate. They get power from the **engine** and transmission.

CAR SMARTS

Power at the Pump

So you're new to driving and you've never pumped gas before. No problem—the automated pumps at today's stations make it super easy. Just pay with a debit or credit card at the pump or inside the station with cash, pop open your tank, and unscrew the cap. Then, push the button on the grade of gas you want, insert the nozzle tip into the gas tank, and squeeze the trigger on the nozzle. Most cars can take low-grade fuel, but consult your manual or mechanic to check whether low, medium, or high grade is right for your car.

ON THE DASH

Now that you've seen what's under the hood and under the belly of your new metallic baby, get inside and look at your dashboard—you know, all those gauges and lights that *aren't* the stereo. Some stuff is really easy to figure out, such as how to activate the hazards or turn on the defrost. But there are a few other important measures, lights, and warning systems that will let you know about the health of your car. Here's what you'll find with breakdowns of what they do.

GAUGES

Speedometer—this measures and displays how fast you're going.

Odometer—a gauge that counts and displays how many miles the car has been driven. It also features a separate counter, called the trip odometer, which you can reset each time you venture out, be it to the mall or to a state park.

Fuel gauge—this indicates how much gas is left in your car's tank.

Temperature gauge—this indicates when your car's coolant temperature is running too hot, too cold, or just right (in which case, the indicator will sit comfortably in the middle).

Tachometer—this gauge shows the engine's speed in thousands of revolutions per minute.

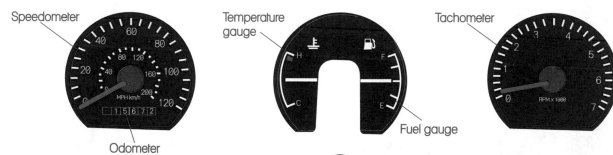

Speedometer

Odometer

Temperature gauge

Fuel gauge

Tachometer

STOCKING YOUR CAR
WITH THE MUST-HAVES

In the same way that you keep an

emergency tampon and a tube of lip gloss in your purse or school locker, you also need to keep some essential items in your car at all times. To prep you and your car for life's little emergencies, put together a Must-Haves Kit to keep in your trunk. Because this tool kit will include big items like a blanket and bottled water, it's best to choose a large canvas bag, a plastic storage container, or even a simple cardboard box that you style out with a few stickers. The idea is to have everything in one place so that you can find the gear you need when you need it. Most can be found at hardware or auto parts stores. If you're lucky enough to have a gearhead in the family, you can even find castoffs lying around your home.

FOR YOUR MUST-HAVES KIT:

AIR GAUGE

There are two kinds of air gauges.

❶ A traditional air gauge looks like a pen with a type of ruler on one end and a steel ball on the other that can be pressed on to a tire's valve. Some gauges have a dial (like those on blood-pressure readers) to display the psi (pounds per square inch), and some have a sliding scale.

❷ A digital air pressure reader is shaped like an electric razor and reads the psi digitally.

What it's for: The air gauge reads how much air pressure is in your tires, alerting you when to add or release air for maximum performance and gas mileage. (See page 60 for instructions.)

Cost: About $10 or less

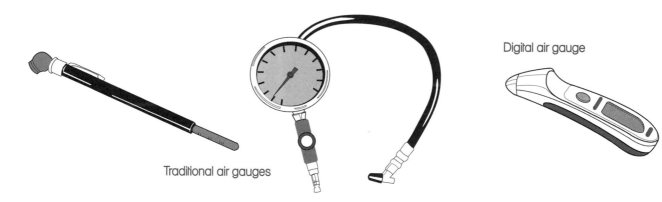

Traditional air gauges

Digital air gauge

BLANKET

A thin microfleece blanket will help you stay warm in a time of need, but it won't bulk up your kit. Also consider buying a waterproof blanket—the slick side keeps dampness out while a fuzzy side keeps you insulated. Some waterproof blankets are equipped with fasteners, so your neatly folded blanket can stay that way, no matter how many speed bumps you barrel over.

What it's for: A simple blanket can be a real life-saver when waiting in cold climate in your locked car for roadside assistance ... or when cozying up with your friends or crush while staring at the stars.

Cost: About $10

ENGINE OIL

 Engine oil is sold in quart-sized plastic bottles and is made in different weights (or grades) and qualities. Common weights (which indicate the oil's ability to move to the engine at different temperatures) are labeled in numbers, like 10-W30 or 20-W50. The "W" indicates that it's OK to use in the winter, and the numbers provide a low and high range of thickness (viscosity) at which the oil will properly flow in cold and normal temperatures. Different cars take different weights of oil. Be sure to consult your owner's manual for the proper type of oil to use in your car.

What it's for: If your oil light illuminates on the dash or if your oil level reads low when you check your dipstick under the hood, quarts can be added to the oil reservoir to ensure your engine is sufficiently lubed for optimum performance. (See page 54 for instructions.)

Cost: $5-$10

FIRST AID KIT

Your first aid kit for the car should be stocked with maps, aspirin, bandages (in several sizes), medical tape, gauze, scissors, instant ice, heat compresses, goggles or sunglasses, a few bottles of water, paper, pens and pencils (for writing down insurance information or leaving notes on windshields), antiseptic, any medications you take, duct tape, and a battery-operated cell phone charger to ensure you have enough juice for emergency calls. Special first aid kits are made just for the car, but you can custom assemble your own for less dough.

What it's for: From treating a minor scrape after a nasty spill on a hiking trail to surviving while utterly stranded, this kit will save you in just about any dicey situation. Bonus: Water will not only help to hydrate your body, but in a pinch it can be used to cool an overheating radiator.

Cost: $50 or less

SCREWDRIVERS, FLAT HEAD AND PHILLIPS

A flat-head screwdriver has a flattened tip and is used for loosening screws that have a single, straight-lined indentation; a Phillips screwdriver has an X-shaped tip. Some screwdrivers are equipped with one type on each end.

What they're for: Screwdrivers are good for adjusting screws on air-filter housing or rearview mirrors. Flat-head screwdrivers can give you an extra bit of muscle when trying to pry apart a stubborn fuse box.

Cost: About $10 each

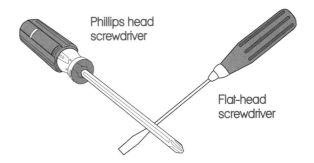

Phillips head screwdriver

Flat-head screwdriver

FLARES AND REFLECTIVE TRIANGLES

Traditional flares have a flame made of magnesium and perchlorates and are about the size of a stick of sidewalk chalk; they burn very brightly but usually for less than 15 minutes and can catch fire in some conditions. LED flares are flameless and look more like Sharpie pens; they burn longer but are not as bright and can be used anywhere because there's no chance of fire. Both are almost always red. It's best to keep four in the car at any time. When using them, place them on the road a few feet from your car.

Reflective triangles are another option. The small, erect signposts are made of durable, weatherproof, reflective bright-orange plastic that can be seen from up to half a mile away and can often withstand up to 40 mph winds. When using them, place them about six to ten car lengths from the back of your car.

What they're for: When you're stuck on the road in the dark, bright-burning flares warn oncoming traffic of your presence.

Cost: $20 or less

LED flare

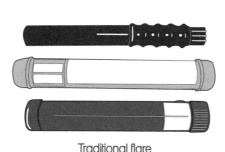
Traditional flare

WOMEN AT THE WHEEL

Women on the Road

The number of women on the road has increased drastically over the past 100 years. In 1910, 5 percent of licensed drivers were women. Between 1940 and 1977, the number of female drivers in the US nearly doubled, as 64 million women became licensed to drive, making up 46 percent of all drivers. And in 2005, for the first time, the number of licensed female drivers surpassed male drivers.

FLASHLIGHT

Unless you'll be spending time examining the underbelly of your car, a compact, lightweight flashlight will do—just be sure you have fresh batteries stashed as well. A headlamp is a great type of flashlight because it is small and gives you hands-free lighting.

What it's for: It's a great help when peeping through the depths of the car—whether under the hood or under the body, or when simply trying to find your other sneaker in that pile in your trunk. It's also useful if you break down at night and need to walk along a dark road.

Cost: $15 or less

JACK

A jack looks like a squashed diamond-shaped piece of metal when stored. It is equipped with an outreaching arm that, when cranked, expands the jack to a true diamond shape. You should always use the jack that comes with your car. If you get a used car without a jack, contact the maker to find out what kind of jack is right for the year, make, and model of your car.

What it's for: A jack will help raise your car off the ground so you can replace a flat tire. (See page 70 for instructions.)

Cost: About $30

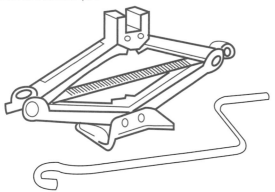

JUMPER CABLES

Jumper cables are simply a set of plastic-coated electrical wires with grippy, spring-loaded clamps on each end. It's a good idea to buy cables that are at least 12 feet long for greater reach from one car to another.

What you'll use them for: Jumper cables resuscitate dead batteries. When your or someone else's car won't start, these wires will take a car from dead to drivable. (See page 77 for instructions.)

Cost: About $25

NEEDLE-NOSE PLIERS

These pliers have serrated insides and sharp, pointed tips, which makes tightly gripping wires and other paper-thin items much easier.

What they're for: They are vital for gripping tiny fuses when swapping out burnt ones. Pliers are also great for loosening stubbornly tight gas caps.

Cost: About $5

RAGS OR PAPER TOWELS

Make sure the rags you have stocked are clean and light in color.

What they're for: Sure, these bad boys will come in handy for wiping dirty hands after messing around under the hood, but clean rags and paper towels are also a vital instrument when checking your oil.

Cost: Cheap. Get some from the store or from your parent's stash at home.

TIRE IRON

A tire iron, or lug wrench, is an oversized criss-crossed or L-shaped wrench. Most often, this tool comes with the car and can be found near the spare tire and jack beneath the fabric lining in the trunk.

What it's for: This tool is essential for prying lug nuts (the thingies that hold the wheel on) loose from the wheel when changing a flat. (See page 70 for instructions.) Criss-crossed wrenches are easier to use, since they enable you to use two hands.

Cost: About $10

WRENCH SET

Open-end wrenches are made with fixed apertures that fit specific sizes of bolts. Check your manual to find out what kind of bolts hold your car together (metric or standard sized) and buy wrenches that will fit those bolts.

What it's for: Wrenches are necessary to loosen bolts on various parts under the hood—like the bolts on the terminal of your battery. They can also come in handy for re-attaching unhinged plastic bumpers.

Cost: About $30

CAR SMARTS

Extras to Consider

To ensure that you have the Rolls-Royce of all tool kits, be sure to add these key items:

✔ **A DISPOSABLE CAMERA**—When some loony driver scrapes up your car, record the damage by snapping a few shots. Old-school film pics are destined to come out sharper than grainy cell phone images. Better yet, if your parents have an old digital camera kicking around, ask 'em for their hand-me-downs—just be sure the battery is charged and the memory card is loaded.

✔ **MONEY**—A little cash can go a long way when you need to cab it to a gas station after you run out of fuel or make a phone call if your cell phone is out of range. Try to keep your kit stocked with $30 or so in bills and coins.

✔ **GLOVES AND HAND CLEANER**—Nothing ruins a fresh manicure faster than tinkering under the hood. Protect your digits from oil and grease with gloves and a heavy-duty hand cleaner.

✔ **SNACK FOOD**—What's worse than being stranded on the side of the road? Being hungry and stranded on the side of the road. Try to keep your kit stocked with nutritional bars, nuts, or dried fruit. And try not to dip into your stash whenever random munchies strike.

5

MAINTAINING YOUR NEW SET OF WHEELS

You know that old saying, "If it ain't broke, don't fix it"? That philosophy sooo doesn't apply to cars. Instead, live by the classic Ice Cube lyric: "Checkity check yoself before you wreck yoself."

Car care is all about preventative maintenance. Think of it this way: If you don't take the time to brush and floss your teeth, you're likely to end up with painful cavities that are also expensive to fix. Likewise, if you don't bother to check your oil regularly, you can end up with a fried engine and a pricey repair job. So just like you have to brush, floss, and get cleanings every six months, you have to check different parts of your car regularly to prevent total system breakdown.

The good news? Maintenance checks are easy to do and take just a few minutes. And fixes won't involve nauseating fluoride treatments or a drill to your dome. Here's how to keep your car's system in check so that your baby will run stronger, longer, and more efficiently.

CHECK THE ENGINE OIL

Tools you'll need: A clean, light-colored rag, extra oil if needed

Time it'll take: Less than five minutes

Why you want to do it: This is one of the most important things you can do to keep your car in good shape. The purpose of engine oil is to take dirt away from the engine and to keep its metal-on-metal parts lubed so they're not grinding against each other. Oil is also needed to keep the cooling system going. If you have an oil leak or your engine is simply burning too much oil, your oil level can fall too low, and your car's health can be in major jeopardy.

How to do it: When the engine is cool, pop the hood (see page 31 for instructions) and remove the dipstick (this one has the oil icon on the handle and is usually located toward the front of the car, closer to the headlights than the windshield). Wipe the end of the dipstick clean with a paper towel or rag. Replace the dipstick in its shaft and remove again—this will give you an accurate reading. The level of oil on the stick should fall somewhere between the "min" and "max" marks labeled on the stick. If your oil is low, use a funnel to add half a quart to the oil reservoir. (Be sure to add the correct type of engine oil to your

ENVIRO TIP

Not So Vital Idle

Like to keep the engine running while waiting for friends outside their houses, or while having long conversations in the car at the end of a night? Not a good idea: The longer you idle, the more pollutants you release into the air. Of course, idling can't be completely avoided—we have to sit at stoplights and wait to make left turns—but to spare the air, don't do it unless it's really necessary.

car—your owner's manual or your mechanic can tell you which you should use.) Check the oil level again and add a bit more if needed. Be careful not to overload your engine with oil—this could damage your spark plugs.

When to do it: If you have an older car, it's best to check your oil once a week; if you have a new car, do it once a month and take your car in for an oil change (the whole reservoir is emptied and refilled) every three months or 3,000 miles, depending on what your owner's manual or mechanic recommends. If you mostly drive short distances, you may need to change your oil more frequently because the engine doesn't have enough heating time to rid the engine oil of water and acids. Above all: If your oil has a burnt look or smell when you check it, it probably needs to be changed.

Road Trip!
The all-girl road trip has long been considered a rite of passage. The 1991 movie *Thelma & Louise*, in which the two main characters drive across the country trying to outrun the cops, immortalized the concept. But the first real women to take on that kind of a trip had a different set of difficulties. In the summer of 1909, a 22-year-old housewife, Alice Ramsey, along with three of her girlfriends, decided to journey from New York to San Francisco by car.

The cross-country trip took nearly two months, and the ladies burned through 11 tires, encountered dicey weather, and had run-ins with unsavory vigilantes before safely arriving at their destination—all without a single map. Ramsey reportedly did all the driving, and in 2000 she became the first woman to be inducted into the Automobile Hall of Fame.

OTHER FLUIDS TO CHECK

Your mechanic may check your fluids when you get an oil change, but it's always good to know where everything is, what it does, and how to know if there's a problem. Some fluids get checked while the car is hot, others when the car is cool. For a refresher on what each fluid looks like and what job it performs, review the Fluids section on page 32 in Chapter 3. To check the fluids, follow the directions below.

CHECK THESE WHEN THE CAR IS COOL:

BRAKE FLUID

Where: The brake fluid reservoir lid is located under the hood on the driver's side.

When: Check it once a month or if the brake warning light comes on. Unscrew or unclip the lid and make sure the fluid level meets the mark on the reservoir.

What to look for: Healthy fluid should be amber in color—not black. Low brake fluid may indicate that you have worn brake pads or a leak, so if your levels are frequently low, have your mechanic check for these or other brake-related problems.

CAR SMARTS

Create an Emergency Car Account

If you aren't blessed with parents who will pay for your car repairs, create a special savings account to help bail yourself out when car care emergencies strike. Do not dip into this account for non-car-related items—no matter how cute those strappy sandals are.

COOLANT

Where: Coolant is located near the radiator in a plastic overflow tank that should have a "full" or "max" marking on its side to help you determine where the fluid level should be.

When: Every year or 12,000 miles

What to look for: Healthy coolant is neon green; if the color seems off, ask your mechanic to change the coolant. If you know you are running low and want to add coolant yourself, be sure to do it when the engine is cool, to prevent pressurized fluid from jumping out when you unscrew the cap. If you notice green- or yellow-colored puddles under your car, it could be that your dog just did its business there, or it could be that your ride is leaking coolant. If you think it's the latter, get your ride to a mechanic ASAP. Driving with no coolant can cause your car to overheat. The mechanic may need to fix a faulty hose, water pump, or radiator to cure the problem.

CHECK THESE WHEN THE CAR IS WARM:

POWER STEERING FLUID

Where: This pinkish-red fluid is in a reservoir located near the belts and is usually marked "power steering fluid" on the cap. Some reservoirs have a dipstick next to it for checking the fluid.

When: If you are having trouble turning the wheel, the problem could be that the power steering fluid is low, so it's time to check it. Routine checks are best to do once a month.

What to look for: Remove the reservoir dipstick and check the level. If your car doesn't have a dipstick, look at the side of the clear reservoir. If it's low, add fluid. If it's always low, you might have a leak—have your mechanic take a look.

TRANSMISSION FLUID

Where: This dipstick will probably be found toward the back of the engine, close to the windshield.

When: Once a month

What to look for: Dunk the dipstick and examine the end. Make sure the level is high enough and that the fluid looks clean (it should be pink, not brown). If your car doesn't have a dedicated dipstick for checking transmission fluid, have your mechanic check the level when you take your car into the shop. A mechanic should flush, or replace, your transmission fluid every 30,000 to 60,000 miles if you drive a stick, and every 60,000 to 100,000 if you drive an automatic.

Note for Newer Cars

On many new cars, the transmission fluid doesn't need to be changed for 100,000 miles or until you need a new transmission. Be sure to check your owner's manual for the manufacturer's recommendations.

CHECK THESE WHEN THE CAR IS EITHER WARM OR COLD:

WINDSHIELD WASHER FLUID

Where: This clear fluid is found in a big plastic tank toward the front of the car.

When: Routinely, as you use your wiper fluid

What to look for: Check the levels against the lines marked on the reservoir and always keep the tank two-thirds full. If you live in a cold climate, make sure the windshield washer solution you use is injected with coolant protection during fall and winter months.

TIRES

TIRE INSPECTION

Why you want to do it: Driving with shoddy tires is like wearing ballet slippers in an ice storm—impossibly slippery and extremely unsafe. To prevent skidding out or blowing a tire, make sure the tread is in good shape.

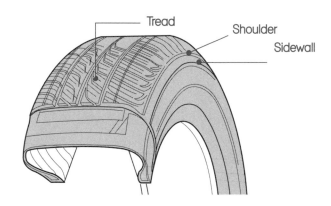

Tread · Shoulder · Sidewall

Tools you'll need: A penny

Time it should take: A few minutes

How to do it: Take a look at your tire and identify the three main parts: the tread (the grooves in the tire that look like the traction on the bottom of your sneakers), the sidewall (the side of the tire), and the shoulder (the rounded part in between). Look closely for unevenness, cuts, swelling, or bald spots on any part of the tires; if you see any of these problems, you may need to shop for new tires. Measure your tire tread by inserting a penny with the top of Abe's head wedged in the grooves of the tire. If you can see the top of Abe's head while your penny is in there, your tire is sufficiently worn and needs to be replaced.

Insert the penny head down into the groove

When to do it: You can check your tires about as often as you take your car in for an oil change—about every three months. For optimum gas mileage, check your tires every month.

CAR SMARTS

Take Care of Your Spare

Be sure to check your spare's air pressure every now and then. The last thing you need when preparing to change a flat tire is finding that your spare doesn't have enough air to do its job.

CHECK TIRE PRESSURE

Why you want to do it: Keeping your tires inflated with the right amount of air not only extends the life of your tires, but also saves you money at the pump. Driving on low tires tacks an extra mile or two per gallon on to your overall gas mileage since the car is working harder to carry the load. Then there's the matter of safety—if you're riding really low, you run the risk that the tread will separate and your tires will blow out.

Tools you'll need: Tire gauge, air compressor (found at gas stations)

How much time it should take: About 20 minutes

How to do it: Eyeballing it is not enough. Tires can lack up to 10 pounds of air and still look like they're perfectly inflated. Grab the tire gauge from your glove compartment or Must-Haves-Kit (see page 44) and unscrew the tire cap on the valve. Stick the round, ball-like end of the gauge on the valve and press firmly (if using a digital reader,

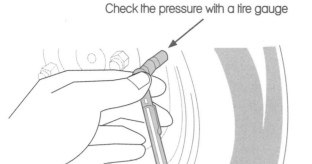

Check the pressure with a tire gauge

When to do it: Check the air pressure in your tires at least once a month. Do it after your car has been parked a few hours to get an accurate reading. Tires tend to lose about 1 pound of pressure each month, and pressure also goes down when the weather gets colder, so be sure to keep on top of your tire pressure checks as the seasons turn.

press it against the valve and wait for the reading on the screen). Compare the reading on your gauge to the psi (pounds per square inch) recommendation found on the inside of the driver's side door or in the owner's manual. Add air with a compressor, which is found at most gas stations. Re-measure the psi and add more air or deflate it a bit (by pressing down on the valve end) if needed. Don't exceed the maximum inflation.

ENVIRO TIP

Under Pressure

According to a survey by the Car Care Council, 54 percent of cars on the road have low tire pressure, causing a 3 percent loss in mileage performance. That means gas gets wasted and more carbon monoxide gets released into the air than is necessary.

CAR SMARTS

Rotation Contemplation

If you really want to get the most mileage out of your tires, have your mechanic rotate them at regular intervals, like whenever you get your oil changed. Rotating them basically means that the mechanic takes off all of the tires and moves them around. Since the front tires usually wear more quickly than the back, swapping them with each other means the tires will last longer. You can also ask your mechanic to rotate your tires at a time when the tires are already off—like when the brakes are getting fixed.

CHECK FUEL TANK CAP

Why you want to do it: Driving around with an ill-fitting gas tank cap is like going on the Tilt-a-Whirl with loose cash in your pockets—you're bound to lose money. When a gas tank isn't fully sealed, pricey gasoline escapes from the tank and evaporates into the air.

How much time it takes: Less than a minute

How to do it: Your gas cap should click a few times when you screw it on. If it doesn't, spring for a new one—the old one is too loose.

When to do it: Any time you pump gas

ENVIRO TIP

Keep It Tight

According to the Car Care Council, nearly 20 percent of drivers motor around with bad or missing gas caps, leaking fuel and contributing significantly to air pollution.

CAR SMARTS

How to Read the Specs on Your Tire

The sidewall of your tire cryptically tells you all kinds of things about your wheels. Here's how to decipher that special code.

Special Code: P215/65R15 88S

P = passenger car tire 215 = the width in diameter of the tire (in millimeters)

65 = percentage of height to width of the tire. Here, the height is 65 percent of the tire's width.

R = radial tire (tires with extra-strength tread)

15 = diameter of the wheel (in inches) that the tire should fit

88 = code number that indicates how many pounds the tire can safely carry (it's not pound for pound)

S = the speed rating code, or how fast the tire can go (an S speed symbol means the car can go up to 112 mph.); speed symbol rating charts can be found online

Your tires will have additional information printed on them, like what kind of materials were used to make the tire, but unless you're part of a pit crew, you don't need to bother with that info.

Special Code

P215/65R15 89H

TIRE NAME

MANUFACTURER

CLEAN BATTERY

Why you should do it: Dirt buildup on your battery can cause it to weaken. If you live in a place with extreme climates, your battery's performance is already taxed by heat in the summer and cold in the winter. What's more, it's overworked thanks to all the phone charging, GPS installing, and stereo upgrading you are likely doing. Removing dirt can help your battery stay juiced.

Tools you'll need: Gloves, goggles, wrench, baking soda, water, paper towels, and wire brush

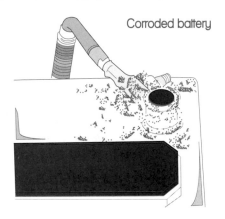

Corroded battery

How much time it should take:
About 30 minutes

How to do it: Put on gloves and goggles to protect yourself from any wayward battery acid that may emit from the battery. Starting with the negative cable (often marked with a minus sign), remove the battery terminals with your **pliers** or **open-ended wrench**. Wipe the top of the case

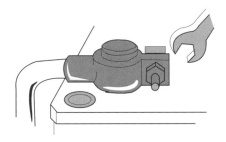

with a damp paper towel. Clean corrosive terminal connections using a wire brush and a mixture of baking soda and water. Next, rinse the battery with a bit of water—just be sure the dirty water doesn't damage the garage or driveway floor (you can throw down a towel or a piece of cardboard to help protect the floor). Finally, re-attach the terminal connections, and make sure they are tight and that the round fittings that surround the screws aren't cracked (if they are, replace them).

When to do it: Clean your battery when you notice corrosive buildup.

Note for Newer Cars

In most newer cars, taking out the battery will disable the stereo system as an anti-theft measure. If you have a newer car, you may need to reprogram your stereo with a four-digit code (which came with the unit) after putting the battery back in.

WOMEN AT THE WHEEL

Driven Women on the Silver Screen

Check out these flicks, in which dames (or, in some cases, dudes dressed as dames) take center stage behind the wheel.

The Cannonball Run (1981)
Thelma & Louse (1991)
Boys on the Side (1995)
Excess Baggage (1997)
Crazy in Alabama (1999)
Rat Race (2001)
Crossroads (2002)
Transamerica (2005)
Herbie Fully Loaded (2005)
Little Miss Sunshine (2006)
Death Proof (2007)

INSPECT AND REPLACE WINDSHIELD WIPERS

Why you should do it: When your wiper blades wear down, it can make for a streaky view of the world—and there's no use in trying to get somewhere if you can't see where you're going.

Tools you'll need: To inspect: nothing. To change: new wiper blades and a screwdriver. You can find wiper blades in auto parts stores or big retailers like Target. To know which ones to buy for your car, read the guide that's shelved in the aisle with the blades.

How much time it should take: About 10 minutes for first-timers, less after that

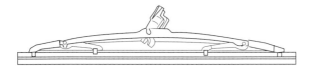

How to do it: Pull the wiper blades in an upright position away from your windshield, then look at the rubber for brittle or warn rubber. If the wipers look beaten up, take a few minutes to replace them.

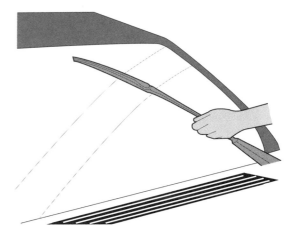

❶ Figure out which blade attachment—pin, tab, or hook slot—you will need to use. (Generally, they are all included in the package.) To determine which one works on your car, simply check what kind of blade attachment is already on your wiper.

2 Release the wiper. Depending on whether your car uses pin attachments, push or pull tab attachments, or hook slots, the method you'll use to release the attachment will vary. If you're working with tab attachments, use your flat-head screwdriver to press the tab on the inside of the attachment. A hook type will also demand screwdriver action to pry the wiper loose. Some types will require you to push a pin in the arm instead. Each method will loosen the blade so you can pull it off and slide the new one on.

3 Slide the new wipers on.

4 Test your wipers. When you're done, be sure the blades are on securely.

When to do it: Windshield blades should be inspected once a month and replaced at least once a year. If you live in an ultracold climate, it's a good idea to change the wiper blades right as winter approaches. (See page 108 on winterizing your car.)

CAR SMARTS

Maintenance Check

Every car maker, manual, and mechanic recommends intervals for when you should check certain car parts to make sure they're working their best. Oftentimes, it is suggested to check the air in your tires and oil every month, check your oil every three months, and do other checks every six months and beyond. To determine what is best for your car, check your manual or talk to your mechanic about when to do certain maintenance checks.

6

FIXING STUFF
ON THE FLY

There are just some things in life every girl should know how to do—like flirt, throw a killer party, and change a tire. It's easy to rely on mechanics to fix everything for us, but there's plenty we can do on our own. Fixing your own car (when possible) not only makes you feel good, but also gives you street cred with your friends and saves money, too. What's more, many repairs are surprisingly simple. Here are some must-know bail-outs and a few bonus fixes to keep you on the road and in control.

CHANGING A TIRE

Getting a flat is a driver's rite of passage. Like getting your period or being dumped for the first time, it happens to everyone at some point (often at the worst time ever) and is almost always a giant pain. The key to gracefully handling a flat-tire emergency is to know what you are doing, so practice changing your tire once or twice in the safety of your own driveway before you are forced to do it in an emergency situation.

Tools you'll need:

✔ spare tire (stocked with air and ready to roll)

✔ jack

✔ air gauge

✔ tire iron

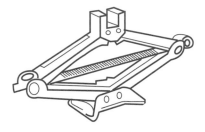

(See Chapter 4 for more on these tools)

Time it will take: If you're a first-timer, changing a tire can take up to 45 minutes, but with experience, you can reduce the time to a quick 10 minutes, usually less time than it takes for roadside assistance to arrive.

How to do it:

❶ **Pull over.** As soon as you feel a flat coming on—you might hear a pop or feel your ride become wobbly—pull over to the side of traffic, out of the way of *any* cars, and preferably to a flat, hard surface. (If your car stops in the middle of the road, put your hazards on and see if you can get someone to help you push it to the side of the road. If you can't, call roadside assistance and wait in the car with the hazards on and the hood up.)

Once you are safely to the side of the road, put the car in park (or first gear if you have a manual transmission) with the emergency brake on and turn on your hazards to warn other drivers of your presence.

2 Get equipped. Grab the air gauge and check the air pressure of the spare to ensure it's properly inflated. (If it's dangerously low on air, call roadside assistance and have them inflate it before it is mounted on the car.)

Find a heavy object to use as a block—like a giant rock or hunk of wood—and wedge it against the opposite tire you're changing. (If you're changing the front driver's side tire, wedge the block behind the rear passenger's side tire; if you're changing the rear driver's side tire, wedge it in front of the front passenger side tire.) This trick will help prevent further slippage.

CAR SMARTS

Roadside Assistance

Even if you become Jane Mechanic, you should always have some kind of emergency roadside assistance service (like AAA or one that is managed through your car insurance). To get this service, you typically need to pay a yearly fee. In exchange you can call them to come and tow your car, jump-start your battery, jimmy your door when you've locked the keys in the car, and change your tire. Bottom line: Every smart girl should have roadside assistance.

③ Remove the flat tire. Affix the tire iron to the tire lugs (the four or five round nuts or bolts that secure the wheel to the hub) and turn counterclockwise to loosen. These suckers are usually on really tight, so you may have to use all your weight to pry them loose.

With the loosened lug caps still on the hub, place the jack underneath the car at a safe jack point. This varies per car, so check your manual for the right location to place the jack. This info can usually be found in the maintenance or emergency sections of your manual.

Raise the car and expand the jack into a diamond shape by turning the hand crank located on the jack. When the flat tire is elevated a few inches from the ground, remove your loosened wheel lugs and stick them in the hub for safe keeping. (Looking for wheel lugs that have rolled away can be about as irritating as getting a flat in the first place.)

Now remove the bad tire. Place it on its side, under the car and near to the jack, so it is positioned as a safety precaution (in case the jack slips or the car falls).

Turn counterclockwise

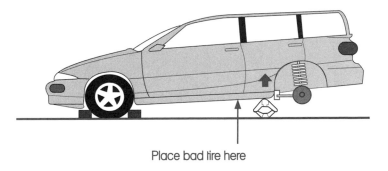

Place bad tire here

④ Install the spare tire. Hoist the spare (the air valve should be facing out) over the wheel studs. This will take some strength; make sure you keep your knees bent and lift the tire with your legs and not with your back. After the tire is on, start putting the lugs back on, first tightening them by hand, then further securing them by using the tire iron. It's best to tighten one lug, then its opposite, working in a star pattern, instead of going in clockwise or counterclockwise order. Using the jack, lower the car back down to the ground. Then tighten the lugs as much as you possibly can, again using all of your body weight, if need be, on the lug wrench. And with that, you're good to go!

When packing up your tools, make sure they're clean and dry so they'll work properly the next time you need them. Finally, go to the mechanic to repair or replace your damaged tire.

TIRE CHANGING DO'S AND DON'TS:

- Don't go beneath the car when it's being held up by the jack. The jack can slip and the car can fall on you.

- Do keep mud, grass, and other yuck out of the rim and hub when replacing a tire. This debris can cause rims to wobble, or cause the wheel to come off while you are driving.

- Don't change a tire while you are still in the way of any traffic.

- Do let drivers know that you're working roadside (so they slow when they pass you and don't spray dirt, gravel, or water). Raise the hood of your car, turn on your hazards, and even put a flare out. (See page 47 for instructions about flares.)

- Don't change a tire on loose gravel or anywhere on a hill—the car can slide too easily when it's jacked up.

ERASE PAINT SCRAPES

Small cuts, scrapes, and bruises are an unavoidable fact of life for a girl on the go. The same is true for your travel-everywhere car. No matter how careful you are, paint chips and small scrapes can happen over time. But with a few simple tools, you can heal your car's little boo-boos.

Tools you'll need:

✔ a small touch-up bottle or paint pen formulated for car touch-ups

✔ a syringe (optional, but helpful)

✔ superfine grade wet/dry sandpaper

✔ fine-cut automotive rubbing compound (a bottled liquid found in auto parts stores)

✔ blow-dryer or leaf blower

✔ soap and water

✔ wax and grease remover

Time it will take: 15 to 20 minutes

How to do it:

❶ **Find the right color.** To find the same shade of paint that the factory used on your car, look for the paint code, which may be located on the sticker of the driver's side door. If you don't find the code there, call the automaker or a local dealer who specializes in your make of car and ask for the color code. You can also go online to touch-up paint retailers and plug in the year, make, and model of your car to find the appropriate color code.

Once you have the color code, you can order touch-up paint in a variety of applications, from paint pens to tiny bottles to spray cans. For pencil-sized scrapes, a paint pen or tiny bottle of paint is best.

2 **Prep the surface.** Before repairing the paint chip or scrape, make sure the area is dry and at room temperature. If you're doing the repair after rainy, dewy, or foggy conditions, dry the area with a blast of hot air (you can use your blow-dryer or a leaf blower).

Next, clean the area with a generous helping of soap and water, and then use a wax and grease remover to fully prime the spot.

3 **Apply the paint.** Once your surface is ready for treatment, use the paint pen to draw over the scratched surface. If using paint from a bottle, try applying it with a syringe—it will distribute the paint in a fine line, giving you control on par with that of a pen. You may be tempted to glop a thick coat over the flaw, but when dispensing paint, less is more.

Apply a few thin coats—like you would nail polish—allowing time for each coat to dry in between (about 15 minutes or so).

Once a few thin layers of paint have dried, use water and a superfine wet/dry sandpaper to smooth out the surface so it is even with the surrounding paint.

Finally, after the surface has dried again, make it shine with a fine-cut automotive compound (a bottled liquid found in auto parts stores). In the end, you'll have a smooth and flawless surface on par with Hollywood's most famous faces after a Botox party.

CAR SMARTS

Like the Pros

It takes an average racing pit crew—usually a team of five or more—6.3 seconds to change two tires. If you find you have a natural knack for the quick change, you may just have a future in the racing scene.

CHECK AND REPLACE AIR FILTER

Tools you'll need:

✔ new air filter

✔ flat-end screwdriver

✔ damp cloth

Time it will take: About 15 minutes

Why you want to do it: An air filter traps debris and dead bugs before they can travel to the engine. When the filter is kept clean, it allows the right amount of air to mix with the fuel that runs your car. If a debris- and bug-clogged filter doesn't allow enough air to pass through to the engine, the car will lose power and run less efficiently.

How to do it:

❶ Locate your air filter; it's the round or rectangular big plastic box under the hood. (See page 35 for a description of it.)

❷ Remove the housing by unlatching the clamps or screws that hold it in place. You might need to use a flat-head screwdriver to pry the clamps open if they've been locked into position for a while.

❸ Slide the old air filter out and inspect it. Is it dirty? Loaded with dead bugs, leaves, and other debris? If so, chuck it and go to step 4. If it looks clean, put it back.

❹ If it needs changing, clean the area where the filter is housed with a damp cloth. Take the new, clean filter and slide it into place. Replace the housing.

When to do it: Check the cleanliness of your air filter every two months.

ENVIRO TIP

Keep It Clean

Keeping your air filter clean will boost your gas mileage by as much as 10 percent, which can reduce pollution and save you money at the pump.

If you notice dirt in only one section of the filter, the filter can be reused as long as there are no cracks in it. Simply remove loose dirt by tapping the filter against a hard surface, then turn the filter around (so both sides will get equal wear) and slide it back in.

JUMP-START A BATTERY

You're rocking out to your newest killer playlist while waiting to pick up your little brother from school. He finally arrives, you turn the key to start the car, and click—you get nothing. What seems like the tiniest infraction—listening to music, failing to shut a car door tightly, or leaving an interior light on overnight—can drain a battery of juice and leave you immobile.

But like the dying hero in any daytime drama, a car battery can almost always be resuscitated in a matter of minutes—you just need the right person around. And lucky for you, a driver with a healthy car battery is easier to find than a devastatingly handsome doctor just waiting to perform CPR. While some cars require special instructions for a jump start (consult your car manual to see if your ride is one of them) most cars are easy to jump-start on your own. Here's how to get the job done.

Tools you'll need:

✔ jumper cables (see page 49 for a description)

✔ another car with a charged battery

Time it will take: About 10 minutes or less

How to do it: The biggest obstacle when jump-starting a battery with jumper cables is finding another driver willing to help you. Once you've found a jumper buddy, follow these three steps:

❶ Make a Connection

✔ First, make sure both cars are in park, turned off, and facing each other. Also be sure that your heater, stereo, and lights are turned off.

✔ If your battery has little caps on the terminals, remove them.

✔ Connect the red-handled, positively charged clamp to the positive terminal (marked "pos" or "+") located on top of your dead battery ①.

✔ Connect the other end of that cable to the positive protruding terminal located on top of the good battery ②.

✔ Connect the black-handled, negatively charged clamp to the negative bolt (marked "neg" or "-") on top of the good battery ③ and connect the opposite end of that cable to a bolt on the engine or on a piece of unpainted metal on your car's frame ④.

Jumper Cable Setup

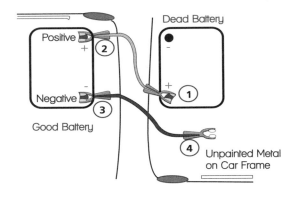

2 Start Your Engines

✔ Have your buddy start the car with the healthy battery.

✔ Now turn your key—your car should start right up.

✔ Once your car is running, disconnect the cables from your car in the opposite order that you attached them, negative (black) first and then positive (red). (If your car doesn't start, you have a more serious problem on your hands—like a completely dead, unchargeable battery or an issue with the starter or alternator, so call roadside assistance.)

3 Drive, Baby, Drive

Be sure to drive the car for at least 15 minutes or so before shutting it off again to fully charge the battery. If the battery is dead the next time you try to start it, you may need to replace it altogether.

CAR SMARTS

Avoid Zaps and Sparks

Don't let your hands touch the ends of the clamps and don't let the ends of the clamps touch one another—these suckers are electrically charged and can zap you.

Also, if you have them on hand, put goggles or sunglasses on before connecting the cables to the batteries to protect your eyes from sparks and wayward battery acid.

REPLACE FRIED FUSES

Fuses are the electrical switchboard of your car. So when a turning signal stops working, the horn falls silent, the dome light inside your car kaputs, or the cigarette lighter no longer charges your phone, it's often the result of a blown fuse.

Your car has its own electrical box that feeds power to every electrical component of your car (just like your apartment or house), and your car's fuse box is stocked with disposable fuses that sometimes go bad. Each of these fuses costs less than a dollar to replace and doing it on your own is easier and cheaper than hauling your car into a mechanic.

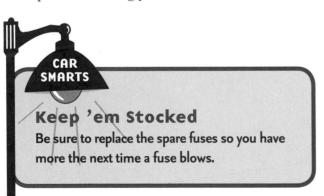

CAR SMARTS

Keep 'em Stocked

Be sure to replace the spare fuses so you have more the next time a fuse blows.

Tools you'll need:

✔ Replacement fuse, which should be stocked in the designated section of your fuse box.

✔ Needle-nose pliers or a fuse puller, which may come with the fuse box.

Time it will take: A couple of minutes

How to do it:

❶ Use your owner's manual to find your fuse box. Some are located under the hood and some are located on the driver's side of the console.

❷ While your car is turned off, pop open the housing and look at the color-coordinated map on the interior lid. This will tell you which fuses control which features in your car. Once you pinpoint the location of the fuse that controls the nonworking electrical part, use your needle-nose pliers to remove the fuse. Look at the fuse closely—if the center wire is burnt or disjointed, the fuse is bad and you can replace it with a new one.

Fuse

Blown fuse

3 To figure out how many watts your replacement fuse needs to be, look at the map again—it should show you the wattage of the fuse that burned out. Remove a spare fuse with the proper wattage (from the spare fuse slots) and pop it into the slot where the old fuse was located. Replace the lid and you're good to go.

CAR SMARTS

Be a DIY Demi-God

If changing a spare or patching a paint job has you itching for more DIY know-how, buy a repair manual for your car. These paperback books contain detailed diagrams and instructions for how to do everything from fix a headlight to take apart your electrical system. Repair manuals are specifically made for each make, model, and year of vehicle and can be found at auto parts stores or online.

CAR RX

When a car's system trips up, there are all kinds of indicators—jarring noises, lit-up warning lights, shaky sensations—to tell us what's wrong. Some problems you can fix yourself; for others you will need help from a pro to fix. See the below chart to know what to do when your car is making weird noises, smells, or movements.

SYMPTOMS	POSSIBLE PROBLEM	WHAT TO DO
Clicking sound when turning the steering wheel	Cracked or damaged CV boot or joint	Take car in to the mechanic
Groaning noise when turning the steering wheel	Power steering fluid is low or power steering belt is loose	Check power steering fluid level and/or have power steering inspected
Squeaky brakes	Brakes are getting too hot from extensive use	Have your brakes inspected by a mechanic
Shrill screech when you make sharp turns or start your car in the morning	Loose belts	Have belts inspected and/or adjusted

FIXING STUFF ON THE FLY

SYMPTOMS	POSSIBLE PROBLEM	WHAT TO DO
Engine backfires (a small explosion occurs in the exhaust or intake manifold due to an imbalanced fuel-to-air ratio and causes a big "pop!" sound)	Problem with fuel injection system	Have mechanic check car
Tough-to-remove oily buildup on the inside of your windshield	Leaking heater core	Have heater core inspected by mechanic
Heat isn't hitting your windshield	Leaking heater core	Have heater core inspected by mechanic
Tread on tires is worn on the outside shoulder OR in the center	Overinflated tires OR underinflated tires	Adjust tire pressure to the correct PSI (see page TK)
Top of the tire looks and feels like fish scales	Worn shocks or struts or wheel alignment is off	Have shocks, struts, and alignment inspected by your mechanic

SYMPTOMS	POSSIBLE PROBLEM	WHAT TO DO
Temperature gauge approaches the red zone (reads hot)	Low coolant level, or problems with the thermostat, radiator, or head gasket	Stop engine immediately and tow to a repair shop
Check Engine light is on	Computer senses a possible problem with the engine or transmission	Check for loose gas cap, which can trigger the light to come on. If light is still illuminated, have your car inspected by a mechanic.
Battery light is on	Alternator isn't charging battery	Check, or have your mechanic check, for missing alternator belt, or have the charging system checked
Oil light is on	Low engine oil level	Stop engine and check engine oil level (see page 54)
Brake light is on	Low brake fluid or problems with the master cylinder or calipers	Check brake fluid—if brake fluid is low, add to it (see page 56), but if it is not low, or problem persists, see mechanic
Puddle of oil on ground under engine	Leak in the engine oil seals, oil pump housing, or pan gasket	Have mechanic check car

SYMPTOMS	POSSIBLE PROBLEM	WHAT TO DO
Overheating (your engine gets too hot and steam or smoke emits from your car)	Low on coolant, problems with water pump, or problems with radiator	Have car towed to a mechanic for repairs (or see page TK)
Headlights are dim	Weak battery or poor electrical grounding	Have mechanic check your battery (recommended every two years)
Car's power is weak when you step on the gas	Clogged or dirty fuel or air filter	Check your air filter (see page 76); if problem continues, have mechanic inspect your fuel filter
Car vibrates when breaking at 40-60 mph	Warped brake rotors	Have brakes inspected
Engine stalls	Problem with fuel filter or spark plugs	Have mechanic check car
Battery won't hold a charge	Corroded battery terminals, low battery, wiring problems, or problems with alternator belt	Have mechanic test battery

Doctors are great, but they don't

necessarily have all the answers. So it's smart if you go into an appointment as an educated patient and know how your body works, as well as what any treatments or prescribed medications will do to you. It's the same with your car. The more you know about how it works, and about various mechanical fixes, the better the advocate you can be for it, yourself, and your wallet when visiting your car's doctor: the mechanic.

With so much information at our fingertips about auto woes (thanks, Internet!) even the most mechanically malnourished Missy can represent herself as an educated customer. And the more knowledgeable you are when communicating with your mechanic, the more seriously you'll be taken. Why get the "girlie" treatment when you should be known as the customer with credibility?

CHOOSING A MECHANIC

Finding the right mechanic is a job in and of itself—not only do you have to find someone with loads of experience who knows your type of car, you want to get someone who will treat you respectfully and honestly and with whom you can build a long-lasting relationship. Your mechanic will be the person who fixes your car when you can't, so it's smart to choose wisely.

So how do you find the best one? Here are some pointers:

❶ Ask your friends and family for recommendations. When someone just *loves* his mechanic, it's probably a good one. Bonus points if it is someone who drives the same make of car (Volvos, for example).

❷ Get online to see what the community is saying about certain mechanics. Sites like *cartalk.com*, *angieslist.com*, and *carrepairratings.com* have a section devoted to customers who rate their own experience with auto shops in cities all over the country.

And no matter how tempting it may be, don't just pick the auto shop closest to your house. While it may seem awfully convenient to be able to drop your car and stroll home, the mechanic closest to you may be more awful than convenient in the end.

Once you have a shop you'd like to try, pay it a visit. You don't need to have a major problem with your car to hit up the mechanic and, in fact, you don't want to wait until your car suffers a complete breakdown to test the waters with a new auto shop.

If your car is due for an oil change or brake check, take it to the shop and see how they do with it. When they're attending to your car, do your own diagnostic. Take the following into consideration.

✔ Is the shop clean?

✔ Did they perform the work at a reasonable price?

✔ Did they charge the price quoted?

✔ Were you comfortable with how the staff treated you?

✔ Did they find a whole lot of unexpected stuff wrong with your car? (If they did, take it to another mechanic before getting it fixed. It's always good to get a second opinion.)

Beth's Auto Service
We Care

Beth Johnson

Phone: 1300 999 9999
Fax: 1300 999 9998
Email:beth@bethauto.com
PO Box 333, San Bruno, CA 94066

If your experience left something to be desired, try another shop until you find a right fit. If you feel good about your experience, be sure to take your mechanic's card and store it in your wallet or glove compartment. And if your new mechanic happens to be 20 miles away, think of the upshot: Some shops offer loaner cars to drive while a customer's car is getting fixed. And it's always fun to bump around in a different car for a day.

HOW TO COMMUNICATE WITH YOUR MECHANIC

Now that you have a mechanic who does right by you and your car, it's time to build a personal relationship with him or her. To get yourself on a favorite customer list, don't bring cookies—come equipped with lots of information about the problem with your car. For example: Say your car makes a screeching noise when you drive it. Don't take it into the shop, mention there's a screeching noise, and expect your mechanic to work magic. Instead, gather as much information as you can about the problem—the more seriously you take your car's ills, the more seriously the mechanic will take you. Ask yourself the following questions:

✔ Does it happen at a certain time of the day?

✔ When did you first notice the problem?

✔ Does it occur under certain conditions (like when you turn, for example)?

✔ Does the problem produce any odors? Colors? Noises? Sensations?

✔ How is the car driving, in general?

✔ Where in the car is the problem coming from?

Also, be prepared to tell your mechanic how many miles per year you drive, whether you drive dirt roads or freeways, and about other work you've had done on the car at other garages in recent history.

Finally, get noisy. A big part of talking your mechanic's language is about being able to *sound* like your faulty car. Does it buzz, whir, screech, bang, or whiz? Can you duplicate the sound yourself? Sure, it might seem goofy to rattle off strange noises, but it's an important part of determining a diagnosis. If you need help describing a sound, check out some of the car noise audio libraries online, like at *autospeak.com*.

SET THE RECORDS STRAIGHT

Before you give your car over to the mechanic, have clear communication with him or her about what the next steps are. Ask about:

✔ their hourly labor rates

✔ whether the repair will require diagnostic tests (and what fees go with them)

✔ what the estimate is for the work

Be sure you are given an invoice with the work slated to be performed (even if all they know upfront is what problem they are investigating). No matter how cool or friendly your mechanic, you'll want to be sure to get everything in writing—it not only protects you and them, but also serves as a great record for the work done on your car (see page 94 on saving your records).

Often your mechanic will need a little one-on-one time with your car to diagnose the problem and give you an accurate estimate for repairs. If you don't have time to sit at the garage while the diagnosis goes down, it's fine to have your mechanic call you with the 411. Before giving verbal consent to fix the car, be sure you understand what needs to be done and how much it will cost—including a breakdown of specific charges for different duties performed. While on the phone, take notes so you can compare your record with the shop's invoice when you return to pick up your ride.

CAR SMARTS

Plead Poverty

If you are really broke, say so! If you tell them you only have the money to fix the absolute essentials, they can tell you what the car needs in order of importance. Mechanics were young once, too. They know what it's like to be a student on a limited income.

WOMEN AT THE WHEEL

First Female Driver

A woman named Genevra Delphine Mudge is considered to be America's first female driver. She reportedly first cruised the streets of New York City in a Waverly electric car in December 1898. The next year, Mudge put her newly acquired skills to the test, driving a Locomobile in a local auto race. Unfortunately, while racing, her car skidded out in the snow, knocking down (but not injuring) a handful of spectators in the process.

AFTER THE WORK IS DONE

When you return to pick up your car, don't just pay and run. Instead, be sure to show up at least 30 minutes before the joint closes. You'll need the time to powwow with the mechanic, pay for the services, and take a quick test drive before the shop closes.

Before you even deal with the bill, ask the mechanic to explain what exactly was wrong and what parts had to be fixed—it shouldn't differ from what was explained before the work was done. Remember to ask your mechanic to show you the old, busted parts and explain how they got that way. Have him point out the new parts or work done on your car. These post-op conversations will teach you more about your car than any manual or book (yes, even this one!), so *really* listen and ask questions if you don't understand something—it's like getting a free lesson (well, with the cost of a repair anyway).

Next, look over your bill and ask questions about anything you don't understand. Mechanics should write out clear descriptions for the new car parts you've paid for, not simply scribble cryptic numbers or codes for those parts.

After you pay, take all your paperwork with you to later be filed in your maintenance records. This will prove invaluable if you have qualms about the work. Creating a file for your car will also help you keep up on your maintenance schedule, reminding you of when you last had new tires put on, for example. Finally, it will serve as a great history for the next owner if you end up selling your car.

When you leave, drive the car around the area for a few minutes to be sure that your squeak, squeal, or thud has been corrected. If something feels weird or the problem is still there, take it back to the mechanic and explain what's going on.

CAR SMARTS

When in Doubt, Get a Second Opinion

Just because your broken-down car is parked at the mechanic doesn't mean you're locked in to getting it fixed there. If the mechanic quoted you one thing, then phoned you with a laundry list of other vital fixes that seem fishy to you, don't be afraid to have the car towed to another mechanic for a second opinion. People do it all the time.

RESOLVING PROBLEMS

If you do run into problems with your mechanic, despite the legwork you've done to select a solid one, it's best to try to work out the problem with the owner or manager of the auto shop. For example, imagine that you've just paid big bucks to have your rotors replaced—and your brakes squeal like a ward of newborn babies whenever you touch the pedal. Check your own hysterics at the door and calmly discuss the problem with the manager of the shop. Request that he or she investigate the work done and explain why the car isn't driving as you expected it to. (It's possible that those squeaks are perfectly normal for the first few minutes of driving or that another ailment that wasn't diagnosed is suddenly rearing its ugly head.) Most mechanics will be happy to take a second look.

CAR SMARTS

Charge It

We all know that paying with plastic can be an addictive and dangerous habit. But when it comes to car repair, charging the repair on a debit or credit card can give you a leg up. Many credit cards offer protection on services done poorly or not rendered at all, and if your mechanic screws something up, the credit card company may fight the charge for you.

NAVIGATING DICEY DRIVING SITUATIONS

Now that you know how your car works

and how to take care of it, you're set, right? Well, almost. You can't forget to take care of yourself, too. Certainly, in driver's ed you were taught to drive safely. But it's important to have some street smarts about driving that go beyond the standard pointers (don't tailgate, don't speed, don't run red lights). Here are a few tips to keep you out of vulnerable positions while motoring into the great wide open.

KEEPING YOURSELF SAFE

⚷ **Be alert.** Be aware of what's going on around you when you're exiting or entering your car. Is there a man sitting in the car parked right next to you staring creepily into space? A woman walking a pack of pit bulls a few yards away? A loud group of drunks coming out of the bar across the street? Survey what's going on all around you and navigate appropriately.

⚷ **Stop where it's bright.** If you need to park, stop for directions, or fill up on gas, do it in a heavily trafficked, well-lit spot. If you have a choice between a gas station that is closed and taking only credit card payments at the pump or one that has a 24-hour quick mart, go to the place that's open and has an employee on site. Park under lights or in spaces closest to the business door. That way, if anything weird goes down, you can rely on employees or customers to have your back.

⚷ **At night or in shady neighborhoods,** drive in left or middle lanes. Vagrants and rabble-rousers are more likely to mess with you at a stoplight or when stopped in traffic if you are close to curbs and sidewalks.

⚷ **Hide your stuff.** Keep any valuables, such as your laptop, iPod, and handbag, out of plain sight—like under a seat—even when you're in the car. Keeping valuables concealed will make you a less attractive target to carjackers and will ensure that you won't forget to hide them once you leave your car for the day or night.

Make sure all your emergency numbers are programmed into your cell phone *and* kept written down somewhere in the car (in your glove compartment with your insurance card is a good place) and on you (on a little card in your wallet) just in case your phone runs out of juice. Numbers that should be on your list are:

- roadside assistance
- insurance company
- family members and friends who could help in an emergency
- police (not just 911, but your local police phone number)

Plan your route. If you're driving somewhere new, plan your route ahead of time (check an online service like Google Maps or ask the people at your destination about the best way to get there) as opposed to just relying on your phone or car's GPS feature, which won't always provide the right information.

Stay alert. When walking to and from your car, forgo fondling your phone or iPod and focus. Have the key for wherever you're going (your car or your house) in hand, so that you can get inside as soon as you get there. Your keys could also be used as a weapon if you need to defend yourself.

Cover your bases. If you're going away for a night or more, give your family your itinerary and license plate number. Arrange check-in times and actually call at those appointed times. Why? Your parents will be thrilled that you are being so responsible (and may give you more freedom in the future), and it will serve as vital information to authorities should you go lost or missing.

Keep it locked. Even in good neighborhoods, remember to keep your windows and doors locked while inside the car—especially at night.

A DRIVER'S WORST-CASE SCENARIO SURVIVAL GUIDE

HOW TO GET OUT OF 6 STICKY SITUATIONS

Fishtailing, rear-ending, carjacking, ugh! Hopefully these things will never happen to you, but accidents do happen and what's more, they happen to teens more than any other group of drivers. The Insurance Institute for Highway Safety has reported that teens are four times as likely as other people on the road to get in an accident because they are less likely than adults to wear seat belts and are more likely to speed, tailgate, and underestimate dangerous situations. Great, right? But you don't need to perpetuate this statistic. If you have trained your brain to cope in a dangerous situation ahead of time, you won't succumb to knee-jerk reactions like slamming the brakes or jerking the wheel, and you'll make safer choices in general. Here's what to do when the unthinkable goes down.

ENVIRO TIP

Go With the Flow

Driving like a Grand Theft Auto character doesn't just increase your chances of injury—it hurts our planet. Aggressive driving can decrease your fuel efficiency by one-third on freeways; and the more gas you burn, the more pollution your car emits into the air. To maximize your gas mileage on freeways, go the speed limit and keep in mind that gas mileage drops the faster you drive.

YOU BLOW A TIRE WHILE DRIVING

POP!

The situation: You're cruising down the highway when you hear a loud pop—your tire has just exploded and you feel as if your heart might, too.

How to prevent it: Keeping your tires properly inflated is the best preventative measure here. Underinflated tires can lead to blown tires. Blazing over potholes and bumps in the road can also lead to blowouts, so slow down or steer clear of them if you can.

If it happens: Yeah, this is freaky, but try not to freak out. Take your foot off the gas pedal and don't slam on the brakes—it will cause your car

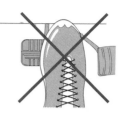

to swerve. Instead, brake very lightly to slow, but not stop, the car. At the same time, strongly grip the steering wheel and, without jerking it, steer to the side of the road. Once you're on the shoulder, continue to press the brake slowly until you're safely stopped. Now take a breath (or 12) and get to changing that tire (see page 70) or calling roadside assistance (see page 71).

YOU GET STRANDED ROADSIDE

The situation: You're coming back from a sun-soaked day at the beach when sputter, sputter…your car slows to a stop. And it won't start up again.

How to prevent it: Everybody's car poops out from time to time. The best way to prevent it is to always keep your gas tank at least half full (running out of gas is a common reason that people get stuck) and to keep up maintenance on your car as best as possible, ensuring your fluid reservoirs are full for long-distance drivers and that your car is running cool. But getting stranded by the road is sometimes unavoidable, so the best thing you can do is simply know what to do if it happens.

If it happens: Use your phone or the emergency phone from your tool kit to call roadside assistance. When waiting for help to arrive, sit in the car with the doors locked. Make sure your hazard lights are on. If for some reason you don't have roadside assistance or don't get cell reception where you are, walk to the nearest business, call box, or pay phone (yeah, they still make them) to get help. No matter how hot, cold, or otherwise miserable you are, resist the temptation to hitch a ride. Instead, walk quickly and confidently to get help. See more safety pointers on page 98.

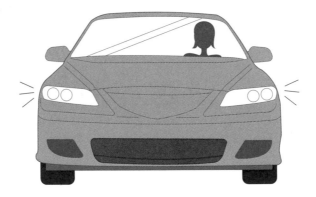

YOUR BRAKES FAIL WHILE DRIVING

The situation: You approach a stop sign, press the brake pedal and ... nothing. You pump the pedal again and again and ... nothing.

How to prevent it: The best way to make sure your brakes are in good working order is to keep up with maintenance checks (see Chapter 5).

If it happens: Slowly release your foot from the foot brake and gently press or pull on the emergency brake pedal or handle. If the emergency brake is also out, navigate your car onto the shoulder. Look for sand, dirt, or mud-covered ground, which will help slow your car to a stop. While you are doing this, downshift a couple of gears to allow the engine to help slow your car. If you have *no other options*, you'll have to collide with something on or off the road. In this situation, it's best to steer in the direction in which you are likely to do the least damage.

CAR SMARTS

Get Defensive With Your Driving

Knowing how to maneuver in sticky situations is vital, but when it comes to enacting what you know, panic can often override logic. So, to be sure you excel in driving through dangerous situations, try signing up for a defensive-driving course. These courses teach you to be a better driver in dangerous situations, like if you have been cut off or are hydroplaning (skidding across the road in wet conditions). In many states, insurance companies even offer a discount for drivers who have completed such a course.

YOU GET INTO AN ACCIDENT

The situation: You're cruising along, windows down and music up when BAM!—you've been hit. Or maybe you hit someone else. Your car is mangled and your nerves are shaken.

How to prevent it: The short of it is: Don't speed or drive erratically, talk on the phone while you are driving, or get obsessed with your iPod. Even if your boyfriend teases you for not going 80 mph on a side street (like he does), keep your driving standards high. It's your car—you drive it the way you want to. That being said, almost everyone has an accident at some point or another.

If it happens: First, make sure everyone in your car and the other car is OK—if not, call 911. If your car is in the line of traffic and you can move it to the side of the road, do so and turn your hazards on. If your car is too damaged or you are in shock, then wait for help to come.

NEXT, YOU'LL WANT TO DO THE FOLLOWING:

✔ Call the police to report the accident. It's best to do this right away, in case the other driver is angry or threatening.

✔ Call your insurance company to report the accident.

✔ Exchange insurance information with the other driver (insurance company, policy number, expiration date, and name). Also, get the driver's license plate number; the year, make, and model of the car; the vehicle identification number (VIN), which can be found on registration papers; the name and address of who the car is registered to; and the person's driver's license number and expiration date (make note if the other driver has an expired or restricted license).

✔ Make notes of damages made as a result of the accident.

✔ Write down the names and phone numbers of any witnesses on the scene.

✔ Grab your disposable camera out of your tool kit and take pics of the damage on any cars involved—this will help significantly when dealing with insurance claims later.

And while you do all this, try to keep a level head—avoid yelling, placing blame, or admitting fault when communicating with other drivers involved. It can all be held against you later on and will only make you more upset.

A Car for Her

In 2004, Volvo designed a car by women, for women called Your Concept Car, which made its debut at the Geneva Motor Show. The car featured: a computerized system to alert one's mechanic of any car problems; a body-scanning system that automatically adjusted mirrors, seats, the steering wheels, and pedals to fit each specific driver; back seats fashioned like those in movie theaters so the bottom portion popped up when not in use, creating more storage room; and a space in the headrest of the driver's seat to comfortably fit a ponytail or updo. While the car was created just for show, Volvo did take the team's ideas to heart and still uses female input when designing its commercial cars.

YOU GET CARJACKED

The situation: You're stopped at a light and see a shady character approaching your car. Or worse, you're parked and gathering your things from the car when someone comes up to your window and threateningly demands your keys.

How to prevent it: Sure, plain old bad luck is a big factor here, but *there are* things you can do to help minimize your risk. First, when parked, don't hang out in your car alone; talking on the phone, writing out that last-minute birthday card, and organizing your gym bag are all things that should be done in a safe public place or at home. When parking your car, choose well-lit places and be aware of pedestrians and other cars around you. While driving, if passengers in cars near you look shady, merge into the middle lane—that way you can't get trapped against the curb at a stoplight.

Finally, when at stoplights and signs, leave enough room between your car and the next to maneuver away from an approaching person if needed.

If it happens: Give the perpetrator whatever objects he or she wants without question—whether it be your car, wallet, or beloved mp3 player/music collection. This move might save your life. After the carjacker flees, call 911 right away. It's likely that in your state of shock, you won't get a good look at the culprit, but try to be aware of height, weight, and skin tone of the jerk who's jacking you. This information will greatly help the police.

CHAP 8

YOUR CAR OVERHEATS

The situation: Plumes of scary-looking smoke rise up from the hood of your car—while you're driving. And guess what? It wasn't your little brother messing around with dry ice again—your engine has literally gotten too hot to handle itself.

How to prevent it: The leading cause of an overheating engine is low coolant levels or busted parts (like hoses, the water pump, or radiator) within your cooling system (see page 37).

Be sure to keep up on your fluid checks once a month and parts checks as recommended by your owner's manual to ensure your cooling system can do its job.

If it happens: Pull over to a safe spot immediately. If you keep driving, you're likely to damage the engine further and create a much higher repair bill—like thousands of dollars higher. So really, pull over. Open your windows and turn the heater on high (this will suck heat from the motor). If, after a few minutes, your car still has more than a three-quarter hot reading on the temperature gauge, call roadside assistance and have the car towed to your mechanic.

CAR SMARTS

Getting Your Car Set for Summer

Your car isn't just a vessel for getting to school and soccer practice, it's your ticket to actualizing the freedom summer represents by helping you get to the pool, beach, movies, and parties. Just like the numbing cold can wreak havoc on your car's heating system, engine, and battery, the sweltering heat can take a toll on your hoses, cooling systems, and air conditioners. Spare yourself the heartache of being housebound on the best beach day—get your car's hoses, battery, and engine oil checked out when summer first starts.

WINTERIZING YOUR CAR

When it comes time to pull out your overcoat, scarves, and winter boots, you should also get your car properly equipped to handle the cold. Icy conditions and freezing temperatures call for extra gear, different types of fluids under the hood, and even altered air levels in your tires. Here's a checklist of how to winterize your car so your baby is just as prepared for the winter as you are.

Refresh your tool kit—In addition to making sure you're well-stocked with must-haves from Chapter 3, add a few winter essentials, like a snow brush or ice scraper for clearing your windows, a small shovel to help dig your way out if you get stuck in the snow, an extra jacket or hoodie for warmth, and a small container of salt, sand, or kitty litter to provide traction when you get stuck on ice.

Upgrade your wiper blades—Windshield wiper blades made especially for winter conditions are heavier and are coated in thick rubber; this is to prevent the wiper parts from freezing and to better clear ice, snow, and sludge from the windshield. Because they're a touch tougher on your motor, they should only be on your car when the conditions call for it. See page 66 for how to install new blades.

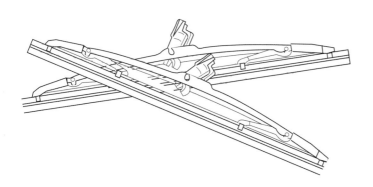

THINGS YOUR MECHANIC CAN DO:

When you take your car into the shop for pre-season maintenance, ask the mechanic to do the following to ensure your car is in tip-top shape for the cold:

Test the battery—Freezing temperatures can cause batteries to lose up to 60 percent of their juice at zero degrees and 35 percent of their juice at 32 degrees and higher so it's smart to get your battery tested to see whether it has the muscle to get you through the winter months.

Alter the coolant—Have your mechanic raise the freezing point of your coolant by adding water to the solution. Your mechanic will know how to trick the solution so that it yields a freezing point that corresponds with that of the climate where you live.

Recognized in Advertising

Though women have been driving since the automobile was invented, many started during World War I (1914-1918) while their husbands were off fighting. But the first auto ads showing women in the driver's seat didn't pop up until the 1920s and 1930s, when American carmakers like Cadillac, Chevrolet, and Ford recognized that a woman's place was not only in the home, but also on the road.

Early ads depicted done-up dames wearing cloche hats, driving gloves, and heels while perched behind the wheel. The accompanying text emphasized style, design, and concepts like "powerful," "dependable," and "velvety operation." The ads also spoke to women as the budget masters of the home, by offering "sensibly low prices."

Change/adjust your oil—Your car may need to run on a different weight of oil than it does in the summertime, so it's a good idea to take your car in for an oil change right before winter (whether it needs it or not) to equip it with the right kind of oil.

Bulk up your tires—Driving in the snow dulls the tread on your tires. If you live in a snowy area, have your mechanic outfit your car with snow tires or snow chains to protect you from slippage. Also, remember that cold weather decreases the air pressure in your tires—make sure to keep checking the psi readings (see page 60 for instructions), no matter how $%#@ing cold it is out there!

Tire with snow chains

CAR SMARTS

Fact or Fiction?

There are lots of myths surrounding car maintenance. Here are a few dispelled.

Q: Can a car engine really explode?

A: Unless you're driving a sports car with highly explosive fuel, no. A car's intake system can backfire or a fuel leak can cause a car to catch fire, but the engine itself won't up and burn.

Q: Can I ruin a car by stuffing a potato or banana in the tailpipe?

A: Not with today's cars. They're equipped with sophisticated computerized systems that sense something is wrong and shut the system down before any damage can occur. In some cases, the exhaust system will simply shoot the banana out of the tailpipe.

Q: Does oil really need to be changed every 3,000 miles (as often as manufacturers say)?

A: Not always. The true test for whether your car needs fresh lube relies on sight and smell, not a number on the odometer. After pulling out the dipstick, wiping off the oil, and redipping the stick, smell the oil that remains. Does it smell burnt? Does it look nearly black instead of a healthy maple color? Then it's time for a change. If the oil looks its natural color, has no burnt odor, and is at the proper level between the min and max marks on the stick, then you don't need an oil change yet. Of course, you don't want to wait too long between oil changes; when in doubt, get it changed.

There is a whole subculture of people who drop crazy loot on pimping their rides with custom stereo systems, hydraulics, flashy rims, and a flurry of unimaginably fancy tweaks. While you might need your hard-earned dough for clothes, travel, or—hello!—college, there are plenty of ways to style your ride without emptying your savings account. Simple moves like cleaning your car and adding a few personal touches will give your car a customized feel and transform it into a comfy home away from home.

KEEP THE INTERIOR CLEAN

If you still live with your parents, your car essentially becomes a mobile home—one of the only places where you have control and complete privacy. Keeping the inside of your car clean can be a chore (like keeping your room clean isn't enough, right?), but it's important to do. Simply put, a clean car makes other passengers feel welcome—how can one *not* feel like they're intruding when they have to crawl over boxes of junk to get to a free seat?

And consider this: Because a car takes you from place to place, it's quite likely that at some point, somebody you want to impress will be in the passenger seat. You wouldn't invite a crush over to a place strewn with dirty underwear and used dishes, right? Keeping your car free of stinky workout clothes and fast-food containers will ensure that when it comes time to motor with the one you like, you'll be ready to do so in style.

ENVIRO TIP

Lighten Your Load

Try to keep your trunk free of heavy, excess stuff. For each extra 100 pounds of junk in yo' trunk, your car's fuel economy is cut by 2 percent.

WASH YOUR CAR

One of the least expensive ways to style your ride is to simply wash it on a regular basis. Aside from achieving that perfect sparkle, keeping your car clean helps preserve the paint job. If you want to do it yourself, it's best to wash your car on an overcast day since the sun causes water to dry quickly and leaves spots. Make sure to hit the underbelly of the car, rinse with plain water before applying cleaning solutions, and vacuum the inside cabin.

WAX ON

Waxing isn't just for bikini lines and legs. And good news—waxing your car is *much* less painful than seeing your esthetician. Every three months or so, boost your car-beautifying routine by waxing your car after you wash it to protect and preserve the paint.

To start, make sure your car is parked out of direct sunlight and apply the wax in small, circular swoops with a sponge. Depending on what type of wax you use, you may need to dampen the sponge before waxing. Like when applying makeup, use a light hand—when it comes to waxing, two thin coats are better than one heavy one.

After you've applied the wax, use a toothbrush to remove any excess wax from nooks and crannies, like keyholes, edges of doors, the hood and trunk, and around emblems. If you want your tires to shine just as brightly as your hood, apply tire cleaner, which is sold alongside wax products in auto parts stores. Finally, you can use an interior wax to protect your dash from cracking under the harsh rays of the sun. All this TLC can take time, so cue up your favorite playlist and make an afternoon of it.

SAVE WATER AT THE CAR WASH

The most eco-friendly and convenient way to wash your car is to run it through a car wash. Surprisingly, mechanical washes use less water than hand-washing jobs; they also have cleaner ways of disposing of washed-off car gunk. Hit up the automated car wash about once a month to keep your car and the local water systems clean.

WHAT'S THAT SMELL?

That clean car smell can go from super fresh to completely rank in no time. Lucky for us, the world of car fresheners has evolved plenty to include several types. Here are some options for every kind of girl on the go.

YOU ARE: An **eco-warrior** who uses chemical-free shampoo and shuns excessive packaging.

TRY: Positioning a satchel of dried aromatic herbs like sage or lavender against one or two of your air vents. The scent of nature will waft through your car whenever your heat or air-conditioning is on.

YOU ARE: A **minimalist** who can't stand to be surrounded by unnecessary do-dads.

TRY: A gel-filled freshener that can stick anywhere on your car, like beneath the dash, where it's out of sight.

YOU ARE: A **gadget fiend** who doesn't trust anything without a power cord.

TRY: An air freshener that plugs into the cigarette lighter in your car. Some even glow neon colors, giving your car a high-tech look.

....

YOU ARE: A **vintage girl** who loves things like vinyl records, second-hand threads, and old-school lunchboxes.

TRY: The iconic pine tree air freshener, hung from the rearview mirror (of course).

Songs to Drive To

A soundtrack is essential when cruising in your new set of wheels, so be sure to create a playlist of autopia-inspired tunes by rockin' women to sing aloud with while cruising. Here's a preliminary list.

"Every Day Is a Winding Road" —Sheryl Crow
"The Rain (Supa Dupa Fly)"—Missy Elliott
"Fast Car"—Tracy Chapman
"Driving"—PJ Harvey
"Cars That Go Boom"—L'Trimm
"Mercedes Benz"—Janis Joplin
"Malibu"—Hole
"Crash"—Gwen Stefani
"Shut Up and Drive"—Rhianna
"Go West Young Man"—Liz Phair
"Driving Sideways"—Amy Mann

ACCESSORIZE

Half the fun of getting dressed for a night out is accessorizing—adding bling, baubles, and the right handbag to perfect your look. So why not do the same for your ride? There are a slew of accessories—from the oh-so-functional GPS device to the bass-heavy stereo—to take your car from plain to personally yours. Here are a few that will help give your car that slick look without breaking the bank.

Plastic floor mats. Though these black or gray mats don't rate high on the bling-o-meter, they will protect the carpet underneath from spills, stains, leaks, rain, and mud. What's best about these buggers is that they're extremely low maintenance. To keep them clean, simply pull 'em out and hose 'em off.

Windshield covers. Yes, windshield covers do have a certain nerdcore vibe to them, but the bottom line is that they protect your dash and interior from the ravaging sun. You wouldn't hit the lake without wearing sunscreen, right? Windshield covers are like sunscreen for your car. Bonus: They also block potential thieves from peering into your front seat and keep the steering wheel cool so that you don't burn your fingers on a hot day.

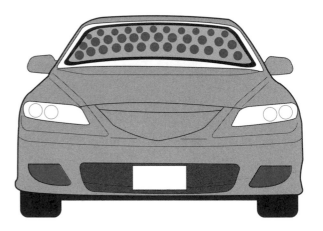

off bad juju. Have a favorite pendant that just doesn't sit right on your chest? Let it liven up your car instead. Into kitsch? Try little fuzzy dice. One word of advice when adorning your rearview mirror: Keep the decorations light and small. Weighty items can smack against and crack your windshield when making sudden stops, and large items can obstruct your view.

Seat covers. So the Lexus with leather seats and individual seat warmers wasn't in the cards, huh? Cover your boring beige upholstery (and the stains from 1996) with fun patterns. Try Hawaiian flowers if you're a beach babe or a Hello Kitty emblem if you're a Harajuku girl.

Rearview mirror ornaments. A quick and simple way to inject personality into your standard sedan is to hang baubles from your rearview mirror. Superstitious? Display an evil eye to ward

Stick shift cover. Add a little hot rod flavor to your ride by throwing a stick shift cover over the boring one installed by the manufacturer. You can scour eBay for everything from cobra-shaped covers to Speed Racer-inspired, leather–clad shifters.

Stickers can signal your political savvy or special brand of humor to everyone who passes your car. Want the world (or at least the road) to know you brake for manitees? Bust out some bumper décor. If you're not one to festoon the outside of your ride with slogans, personalize the interior with smaller decals of your favorite bands, skate company, or cartoon characters—the underbelly of the glove compartment and spaces along the dash are a good place to start. One caveat to keep in mind when you peel the backing off of that Kelly Clarkson sticker: Consider how your décor will affect your car's resale value. After all, not every potential buyer will like Ms. Clarkson as much as you do (heck, *you* might not even like her a few years from now).

GIVE YOUR CAR A HANDBAG

After all the work you do to ensure your car stays healthy and well-equipped for emergencies, it's important to remember that having a car is also about having fun. So why not style your ride with a custom bag filled with rockin' goodies for the road? Grab a roomy bag—like your dad's retired gardening bag with all those outside pockets— and fill it with the things you might need when cruising around.

For example, if you're a water baby, keep a swim-suit, towel, sunscreen, book, and bottle of water in your bag for impromptu trips to the beach. If you're an art fiend, keep a small canvas, paint, brushes, and smock in your bag—you never know when you might be inspired to pull over and re-create that perfect landscape. Maybe you love hosting parties. Stock your bag with picnic sup-plies, portable iPod speakers, and a deck of cards. The next time you and your friends are driving around with nothing to do, you can take a quick trip to the market and then create a killer spread in an area park. No matter what your passion, this handbag for your car will find you prepared for anything.

KEEP THE LOVE ALIVE

You may be excited to take care of and prettify your car when it's new to you, but over time you might lose interest in keeping it happy and healthy. It's one thing to let your once-favorite hoodie become stinky gymwear; it's another to stop loving your car. Whether you plan to have this car for six months or six years, it's still the only first car you'll ever have. Treat it well, and it will provide you with some of your best memories. Plus, you'll be able to fetch a top asking price whenever you decide to upgrade to that classic drop-top or off-roader.

A

accessories, 118–120
accidents, 100, 104–105
air filters, 35, 76–77
air fresheners, 116–117
air gauges, 44
alternator, 35
anatomy overview, See
        also specific parts
        and systems,
        29–31.
axles, 38, 40

B

battery
    charging, 35
    cleaning, 64–65
    described, 37
    jump-starting, 77–79

testing, 109
belts, 35
blankets, 45
Blue Book, 20
body work, 16, 17
brake (hydraulic) fluid,
        32, 56
brake system, 38–40, 103

C

calipers, 39
camera, disposable, 51
carjackings, 106
catalytic converter, 36,
        38
checkup, paying for, 12
cleaning, 114–116
comfortable, getting, 19
Consumer Reports, 20

contracts, 22
coolant, 33, 57, 109
cooling system, 37
cost estimation, 12–13,
        20
CV boot, 36

D

dashboard, 41
defensive-driving
        courses, 103
differential, 40
drive belts, 35

E

emergency tool kits,
        43–51, 108
engine
    checking, 16

diagram, 38
idling, 55
myths, 111
overview, 34–37
engine oil, 33, 45, 54–55
exhaust manifold, 36
exhaust pipe, 36, 38–39
exhaust system, 39, 111

F

first aid kit, 46
flares, 47
flashlights, 48
floor mats, plastic, 118
fluids, 32–34
frame, 38, 40
fresheners, 116–117
fuel
    efficiency, 100, 114

filter, 36
gauge, 41
injector, 36
paying for, 12
pumping, 40
tank cap, 62
fuses, replacing, 80–81

G
gas, see fuel
gloves, 51
GPS feature, 99
Green Vehicle Guide, 14

H
handbag, 120–121
hand cleaner, 51
hood, popping, 31
hoses, 36, 37
hydraulic (brake) line, 40

I
inspection, 16–17, 21
insurance, 12, 23, 103
intake manifold, 36

J
jacks, 49
jumper cables, 49

K
Kelley Blue Book, 20

L
license/registration, 12
liens, 21
loan basics, 13
lug nuts, 50, 72, 73

M
maintenance
    mechanic tasks, 109–
        110
    myths, 111
    overview, 53–67
    records, 92–94
    summer, 108
    winter, 108–109
master cylinder, 40
mechanics. See also
        repairs
    choosing, 88–90
    communicating with,
        90–94
    maintenance tasks,
        109–110
    overview, 87

problem resolution,
    95
mirror ornaments, 119
money, 51, 56
Mudge, Genevra
        Delphine, 93
muffler, 36, 38, 39
Muldowney, Shirley, 27

N
numbers, emergency, 99

O
odometer, 41
oil, changing, 110, 111
overheating, 107
owner's manuals, 25–27,
    72

P

paint (color) code, 74

paint scrapes, erasing, 74–75

pliers, needle-nose, 49

power-steering fluid, 34, 57

power-steering pump, 37

purchase
  buying process, 22
  insurance, 12, 23
  overview, 11–23
  research, 18, 20–21
  of used cars, 15–17, 20

R

radiator, 36, 37

rags, 50

Ramsey, Alice, 55

reflective triangles, 47

registration, 12

repairs. See also
    mechanics
  air filters, 35, 76–77
  battery, jump-starting, 77–79
  estimates, 92
  fuses, replacing, 80–81
  manuals, 81
  overview, 69
  paint scrapes, erasing, 74–75
  paying for, 12, 56, 92, 95
  second opinions, 89, 94

tires, changing, 70–73

troubleshooting, 82–85, 91

research, 18, 20–21

roadside assistance, 71

rotors, 39, 40

rubbing compound, 74, 75

S

safety
  accidents, 100, 104–105
  brakes, failure of, 103
  carjackings, 106
  checking, 20
  checklist, 98–99
  overheating, 107
  overview, 97
  stranded, procedure, 102
  tires, blowing, 101

screwdrivers, 46

seat covers, 119

second opinions, 89, 94

selection. See purchase

shocks, 16, 38, 39

snack food, 51

snow chains, 110

speedometer, 41

stickers, 120

stick shift covers, 120

stranded, procedure, 102

struts, 38, 39

T

tachometer, 41

taxes, 15, 22

temperature gauge, 41
test-driving, 17–18, 93
thermostat, 37
tire iron, 50
tires
    blowing, 101
    changing, 70–73
    maintenance of, 59–63
    used, inspection of, 16
    winterizing, 110
transaxle, 37
transmission, 37, 38
transmission fluid, 34, 58
troubleshooting, 82–85,
    91

U
Used Car Buying Guide,
    20

used cars, purchasing,
    15–17, 20

V
Volvo, 105

W
warranties, 22
water pump, 37
waxing, 115
windshield covers, 118
windshield washer fluid,
    32, 58
windshield wipers, 66–
    67, 109
women drivers, 18, 48,
    93, 110

women inventors, 33
wrench set, 50

Y
Your Concept Car, 105

ABOUT THE AUTHOR

ERIKA STALDER is a San Francisco-based writer who has contributed to *Wired*, *Missbehave*, *Planet*, and *The Journal of Life Sciences*, and worked with the International Museum of Women to produce the *Imagining Ourselves* anthology. She also currently writes the Dear Erika advice column for ABC Family's The Secret Life of the American Teen website. Her other books include Zest Books' *Fashion 101*, *The Date Book*, and *97 Things to Do Before Your Finish High School*.

ACKNOWLEDGEMENTS

Thanks to my patient editor Karen Macklin, the crew at Zest Books, and the Zest Teen Advisory Board for all of their help in producing this book. I'd also like to thank the peeps who helped teach me about cars, especially Bill Mufarrah at B&W Service in San Francisco, Kenny Bezzant, and my pops. And my gratitude to the following for their inspiration and support: Deborah Brosseau, Danielle Farrar, Beth Kita, Diane Kwan, Grant G. Lee, Lisa Lemen, Pro-Photo, Alicia Mangiaracina, William Rhett Marzett from Bank of the West, Miracle, Melissa Miller, Eleni Nicholas, Erin Reedy, Ben Rojas, Christina Rondeau, Rachel Shaw, Rebecca Smith Hurd, and Jo Stalder.